Lizard

Animal
Series editor: Jonathan Burt

Already published

Albatross Graham Barwell · *Ant* Charlotte Sleigh · *Ape* John Sorenson · *Badger* Daniel Heath Justice
Bear Robert E. Bieder · *Beaver* Rachel Poliquin · *Bee* Claire Preston · *Beetle* Adam Dodd
Bison Desmond Morris · *Camel* Robert Irwin · *Cat* Katharine M. Rogers · *Chicken* Annie Potts
Cockroach Marion Copeland · *Cow* Hannah Velten · *Crocodile* Dan Wylie · *Crow* Boria Sax
Deer John Fletcher · *Dog* Susan McHugh · *Dolphin* Alan Rauch · *Donkey* Jill Bough
Duck Victoria de Rijke · *Eagle* Janine Rogers · *Eel* Richard Schweid · *Elephant* Dan Wylie
Falcon Helen Macdonald · *Flamingo* Caitlin R. Kight · *Fly* Steven Connor · *Fox* Martin Wallen
Frog Charlotte Sleigh · *Giraffe* Edgar Williams · *Goat* Joy Hinson · *Gorilla* Ted Gott and
Kathryn Weir · *Guinea Pig* Dorothy Yamamoto · *Hare* Simon Carnell · *Hedgehog* Hugh Warwick
Hippopotamus Edgar Williams · *Horse* Elaine Walker · *Hyena* Mikita Brottman · *Kangaroo* John Simons
Leech Robert G. W. Kirk and Neil Pemberton · *Leopard* Desmond Morris · *Lion* Deirdre Jackson
Lizard Boria Sax · *Llama* Helen Cowie · *Lobster* Richard J. King · *Monkey* Desmond Morris
Moose Kevin Jackson · *Mosquito* Richard Jones · *Moth* Matthew Gandy · *Mouse* Georgie Carroll
Octopus Richard Schweid · *Ostrich* Edgar Williams · *Otter* Daniel Allen · *Owl* Desmond Morris
Oyster Rebecca Stott · *Parrot* Paul Carter · *Peacock* Christine E. Jackson · *Penguin* Stephen Martin
Pig Brett Mizelle · *Pigeon* Barbara Allen · *Rabbit* Victoria Dickenson · *Rat* Jonathan Burt
Rhinoceros Kelly Enright · *Salmon* Peter Coates · *Scorpion* Louise M. Pryke · *Seal* Victoria Dickenson
Shark Dean Crawford · *Sheep* Philip Armstrong · *Skunk* Alyce Miller · *Snail* Peter Williams
Snake Drake Stutesman · *Sparrow* Kim Todd · *Spider* Katarzyna and Sergiusz Michalski
Swallow Angela Turner · *Swan* Peter Young · *Tiger* Susie Green · *Tortoise* Peter Young
Trout James Owen · *Vulture* Thom van Dooren · *Walrus* John Miller and Louise Miller
Whale Joe Roman · *Wild Boar* Dorothy Yamamoto · *Woodpecker* Gerard Gorman · *Wolf* Garry Marvin

Lizard

Boria Sax

REAKTION BOOKS

To the dinosaurs,
past, present, and yet to come . . .

Published by
REAKTION BOOKS LTD
Unit 32, Waterside
44–48 Wharf Road
London N1 7UX, UK
www.reaktionbooks.co.uk

First published 2017
Copyright © Boria Sax 2017

Printed and bound in China by 1010 Printing International Ltd

A catalogue record for this book is available from the British Library

ISBN 978 1 78023 828 9

Contents

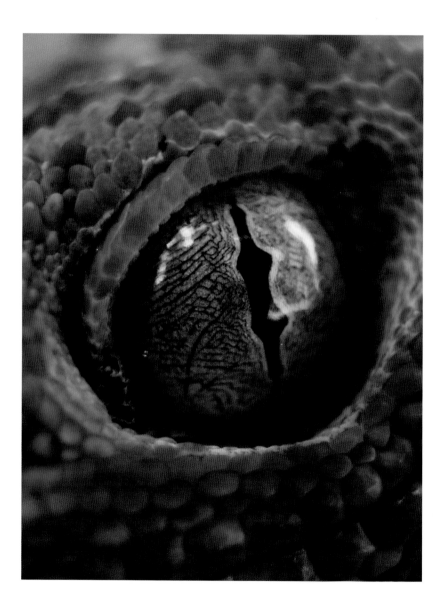

1 What is a Lizard?

To write a poem is like trying to catch a lizard without its tail falling off.
Lawrence Durrell

'Charismatic megafauna' such as tigers, elephants and pandas command our attention, but lizards have an even greater ability to inspire fantasy. We vastly increase their size, bestow wings upon them and make them exhale flame. Our storybooks are full of lizards, but we usually call them something else – dragons, serpents, dinosaurs, monsters. Lizards are at once overhyped and underappreciated. Perhaps we might compare them to contemporary celebrities, who are worshipped almost as deities, and not allowed to be 'human'. Movie stars cannot walk to the corner shop without having new photographs of them posted on the Internet, after which fans will comment on their clothes, weight and companions. Finding the man or woman in a celebrity is a bit like finding the lizard in a dragon.

What is a 'lizard'? The name generally evokes a small, slender creature with a very lithe body and an extended tail. That is usually fairly accurate, though the Komodo dragon, found on a few islands in Indonesia, can grow to about 3 m (10 ft) in length. The short-horned lizard of the American Southwest and Mexico is thick around the middle, and has often been taken for a toad. As we will explain in more detail later, lizards have a very wide range of patterns and colours, and many can even change colour according to their moods or environments. Some also have a variety of tufts, frills, crests, spikes, dewlaps (throat pouches) or horns. Some can reproduce asexually, and some have a vestigial third, or parietal, eye. Many, when pursued, can cast off part of their tails, which then continue to writhe, distracting potential predators. A few can walk on two feet and even scurry across water. They are so diverse that almost anything can seem possible with them. Because the boundaries of the category appear so broad and flexible, creatures from tadpoles to scorpions have been designated as 'lizards' in the past.

In books from the ancient world, it is never possible to know for sure exactly what species a word refers to. In the Jerusalem translation of the Bible, numbered among the creatures that are 'wisest of the wise' is 'the lizard, which you can catch in your hand, yet . . . frequents the palaces of kings' (Proverbs 30:28). Here, the Hebrew word *semamit* is translated as 'lizard', but many other translations, including the King James Bible, use 'spider'.[1] Translators of Aristotle generally render his word *saurion* as 'lizard', but his meaning was certainly far more specific. He was probably referring primarily to wall lizards, which are common in Greece, and perhaps to any creatures that closely resembled them.

Our word 'lizard' is one of many terms for animals that entered the English language through Norman French. It comes from the Gallic *lesard*, which is derived from the Latin *lacertus*, meaning 'muscle'. The connection is uncertain, but perhaps it derived from the shape of the animal, thicker in the middle and tapering at the ends. In analogous cases, the indigenous English word for an animal often became a term for the living creature, while the French word designated the animal as a food. Accordingly, we use the Old English 'pig' and 'steer' or 'cow' to speak of creatures of the farmyard, while 'pork' and 'beef', words from the Old French, designate what they become on the dinner table. But, since lizards are not widely eaten outside of some areas of Latin America, Africa, the Near East and Oceania, that was not a possibility for them.

1.) *Das Chamäleon* (Chamaeleon mitratus.)
2.) *Der Drache* (Draco volans.) 3.) *Der gefleckte Gecko* (Platydactilus guttatus.)

The word 'lizard' became one of many near-synonyms for animals that creep or glide, which were then loosely distinguished mostly by associations – for example 'serpent', 'stellio', 'sauria' and 'dragon'. Almost no attempt was made to standardize these categories or make them mutually exclusive. One thirteenth-century English bestiary tells us, 'There are many kinds of lizards, such as the botrox [probably a tadpole], the salamander and the newt.'[2] As it happens, all three of those animals are now considered amphibians.

To a large extent, the classification of human cultures was the model for biological taxonomy, and authors did not hesitate to include moral and social factors among their criteria. It has been common in Western culture to pair off two varieties of animal that are then defined in contrast to one another, almost invariably to the detriment of one party: the dove of peace and the raven of doom, the loyal dog and the savage wolf, the cute mouse and the vicious rat. In a similar way, the lizard was sometimes contrasted with the snake.

Much of the time, the two creatures were referred to collectively as 'serpents'. Snakes, however, are much more likely than lizards to be venomous. Many snakes eat mammals, while lizards, with a few exceptions, stick to invertebrates. Furthermore, snakes lack eyelids, but most lizards have lids that close from below, softening their gaze. The stare of a snake appears far more intense and menacing, and there are many stories of them being able to kill or hypnotize their prey with a glance alone. The English clergyman Edward Topsell, in a work published in the mid-seventeenth century, stated that lizards were distinguished from other serpents by their friendliness to human beings. When people would sleep in open fields, malignant snakes would try to enter their mouths, but lizards would warn them by scratching on their cheeks. The evil reptile here is obviously a slightly secularized image of the Devil, while the good one was a sort of guardian angel. The cleric had in mind primarily the green lizard, a lacertid that is fairly common in much of Southern Europe. Elsewhere, however, Topsell listed the crocodile and scorpion as lizards, animals that certainly did not have a benign reputation.[3]

When classification of animals gradually became more systematic, the place of lizards was a special cause of perplexity. Oliver Goldsmith wrote in his *History of Animated Nature*, first published in 1774,

> It is indeed no easy matter to tell to what class in nature lizards are chiefly allied. They are unjustly raised to the rank of beasts, as they bring forth eggs, dispense with breathing, and are not covered with hair. They cannot be placed among fishes, as the majority of them live on land; they are excluded from the serpent tribe by their feet, upon which they run with some celerity, and from insects by their size, for though the newt may be looked upon in this contemptible light, a crocodile would be a terrible lizard indeed. Thus lizards are excluded from every rank, while they exhibit somewhat of the properties of all.[4]

Lizards, in other words, were a puzzle that almost threw the whole prospect of systematically classifying animals into disarray. They appeared to be a sort of microcosm of the entire animal world.

This made lizards, at least in Western culture, what the anthropologist Mary Douglas called 'obscure, unclassifiable elements that do not fit the pattern of the cosmos'.[5] According to her theory, such creatures are accorded mysterious powers, which hover between holiness and abomination, by human cultures. But lizards have generally been credited with far less of a numinous quality than snakes, which are relatively consistent in appearance and offer no great challenge to taxonomists. Every snake in Western culture is associated with the biblical serpent in the Garden of Eden, but there is no comparably iconic figure for lizards.

This contrast appears to extend beyond the Occident, and, in cultures of the world, lizards, unlike snakes, are often a 'covert taxon', a category of creatures that are associated with one another yet not given an explicit name.[6] Nevertheless, with a few modifications, Douglas's theory may turn out to be largely correct after

J. J. Grandville, illustration from *Scènes de la vie privée et publique des animaux* (1842). The snake is placed on trial by the animals for killing a toad. It is contrasted with the 'civilized' lizard directly in front of it.

Plus on avance , moins on pénètre l'horrible mystère dont l'infortuné crapaud a été victime.

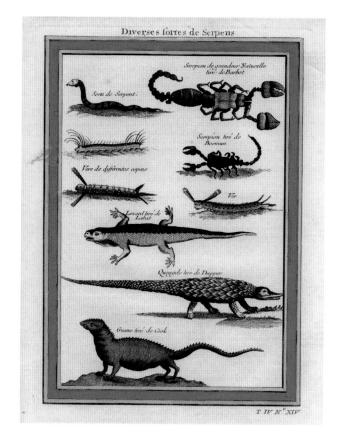

all. Precisely because lizards do not call forth very consistent images or associations, their representation has required more inventiveness, and they have inspired a wider range of mythological figures than perhaps any other animal. The dragon is an amalgamation of many lizards into a single figure.

One reason why it has proved so difficult to classify lizards is because evolutionary kinship is not always a very good indicator

Two mosaics from the 81st Street subway station in New York, next to the American Museum of Natural History. The first shows a basilisk lizard with a *Tyrannosaurus rex* in the background; the second, a snake against the tail of a dinosaur. Animals of today are haunted by their precursors. These mosaics are a reminder of how the same forms reappear often among living things.

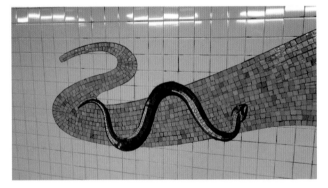

of the appearance or habits of an animal. Because of biological convergence, animals that are not closely related, though often in analogous environments, may develop similar features. Accordingly, bats, birds, butterflies, flying fish and gliding lizards soar with wings, even though they belong to different biological categories. Porpoises and whales have much the same appearance as fish. Crows, parrots and porpoises rival the great apes in intelligence. Both salamanders and chameleons shoot out their tongues with great speed and power at insects, at about half the length of their bodies or more (with chameleons, much more), and then reel the prey into their mouths. Lineage is only one type of kinship and not always the most important.

The basic appearance of a lizard has appeared many times in evolution, among dinosaurs, amphibians and modern reptiles. It is even found occasionally among mammals. One example is the pangolin, a scaly, tree-climbing anteater that is found in parts of Africa, Asia and the Philippines. Another such mammal is the armadillo, found in the Americas, which has a hard, patterned shell that resembles scales, as well as a long, tapering tail. So should we call a pangolin or armadillo a 'lizard', as the people in the eighteenth and early nineteenth centuries sometimes did? Taxonomy of animals, like all classifications, is a matter of utility rather than truth or falsity, so the answer depends on our purposes. There is nothing fundamentally illogical about classifying the pangolin as a lizard, but that categorization is based on form rather than evolutionary inheritance.

Linnaeus had grouped reptiles and amphibians together in a single class – *amphibia*. The importance of the distinction between them became apparent to biologists only in the early nineteenth century. They were first placed in distinct categories by the French biologist Pierre André Latreille in 1825, and soon afterwards by Richard Owen, Thomas Henry Huxley and others. This meant that the creatures that had formerly gone by the name of 'lizard' were abruptly split into two groups. About half of lizards, the amphibians, were, so to speak, suddenly 'excommunicated'.

This opened a gap between scientific terminology and common perception that was even greater – and appeared far more abruptly – than when zoologists decided to consider cetaceans as mammals rather than fish. Both changes in classification anticipated the Darwin–Wallace theory of evolution, which, though

Illustration to G. H. von Schubert, *Natural History of the Animal Kingdom for School and Home* (c. 1869). People of the Victorian era were fascinated by anomalies, animals that did not fit neatly into conventional classifications. Clockwise starting in the upper left corner, we have five such creatures – an armadillo, a sloth, a platypus, a giant anteater and a pangolin.

Illustration to Oliver Goldsmith, *History of Animated Nature* (1774). The armadillo was initially taken for a lizard at times because of its long tail and scales. Although it is a New World animal, this one is placed beside the ruins of a Graeco-Roman temple, perhaps to illustrate the transience of earthly grandeur and the permanence of nature.

not entirely unprecedented, would soon become the focus of an ongoing tension between faith and science. Particularly in the ambience of the latter nineteenth and early twentieth centuries, naive perception would usually be aligned with religion, even though Christianity, like science, was filled with esoteric concepts. Herman Melville had expressed something of the sort in *Moby-Dick*, when he invoked the 'holy Jonah' in arguing that the whale was a fish.[7]

When Linnaeus published the first edition of his *Systema naturae* in 1735, taxonomy went from being a casual, relatively informal activity to a highly contested branch of science. Biologists from the mid-nineteenth century on divided up the animal kingdom in many ways, but nearly all of them placed reptiles and amphibians in separate categories, and the differentiation has persisted to this day. Amphibians generally undergo a metamorphosis, such as that of a tadpole to a frog. They spend part of their

De Seve del.   Jsc Taylor sculp.

The Armadillo.

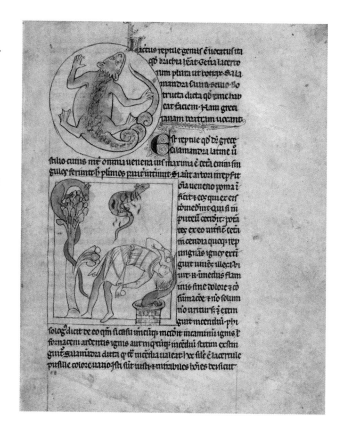

A Lizard and Salamanders, England, 1250–60, manuscript illustration. Here the lizard (above) is a creature of water, while the salamanders (below) were believed to be creatures of fire. One of the salamanders gives off flames, and a man recoils from the heat.

lives in water, breathing through gills, and part on land, breathing with lungs. Reptiles live mostly on land and breathe only through lungs. The skins of amphibians are generally smooth, moist and permeable to water, while those of reptiles are dry and usually covered with scales. In terms of evolution, reptiles are actually far more closely related to mammals than to amphibians.

For the lay observer, however, the similarities between many amphibians and lizards are more dramatic than the differences.

Both, for the most part, have elongated, sinuous bodies that fade into extended tails. They are ectothermic (cold-blooded), and generally keep their bodies close to the ground, where they move by creeping or sliding, progressing forward in rhythmic, undulating curves. Even today, both types of animals are studied together in a single field – herpetology. The remarkable resemblance of a gecko to a salamander, however, is not an instance of convergence like that of a fish and a whale, since the basic morphology of the cold-blooded pair probably goes back to a common ancestor that lived when reptiles diverged from amphibians about 320 million years ago. What is noteworthy in this case is not that reappearance of a basic form, but the fact that one should persist relatively unchanged for such an immense amount of time.

The placing of reptiles and amphibians in separate categories did not cause a great stir. Although it challenged the Linnaean

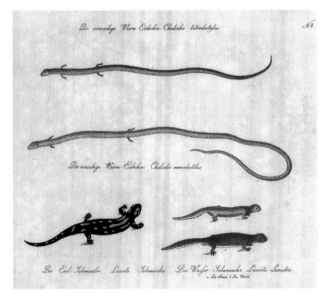

Illustration to *Naturhistorische Bilder Gallerie aus dem Tierreich* by J. C. Brodtman (1816). Here, skinks and salamanders are classified together, perhaps because they both have highly flexible bodies.

'Reptiles', from a book of natural history, 1860. When this picture was made, the taxonomic distinction between reptiles and amphibians was still disputed among taxonomists. The animals classed as reptiles here include two snakes, two lizards, two frogs, one toad and three salamanders.

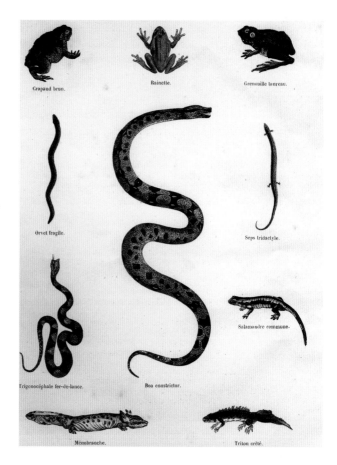

Crapaud brun.

Rainette.

Grenouille taureau.

Orvet fragile.

Seps tridactyle.

Salamandre commune.

Trigonocéphale fer-de-lance.

Boa constrictor.

Ménobranche.

Triton crêté.

division of animals into discrete units that had been fixed for eternity by God, it seemed to be in harmony with an alternative paradigm for ordering the natural world. This was 'the great chain of being', in which organisms were primarily organized vertically rather than horizontally, in an ever-increasing scale of perfection, culminating – among terrestrial creatures – in humankind, but

Illustration by Adolphe Millot to *Nouveau Larousse illustré* (1897–1904). By the end of the 19th century, the distinction between reptiles and amphibians had been widely accepted by zoologists for several decades, but many publications did not always observe it. Here frogs and salamanders are still included among the reptiles.

ultimately embracing the angels, archangels and God. According to this model, the boundaries between varieties of animals were always fluid, and categories blended into one another. Near the end of the eighteenth century, Thomas Pennant wrote of the pangolin, 'These animals approach so nearly the genus of lizards, as to be links in the chain of beings which connect proper quadrupeds with the reptile class.'[8] Various intellectual systems

'The Pangolin', illustration to *History of Animated Nature* by Oliver Goldsmith (1774). Goldsmith classified the pangolin, together with the armadillo, as 'animals of the scaly kind'. He remarked that it was usually considered a lizard, but gave birth to live young like a mammal.

Vol. IV.

Page 119.

De Seve del.

Ifⁱᵉ Taylor sculp.

The Pangolin.

– some quite complex – attempted to combine the two paradigms, and these involved positing a hierarchy of categories, running from vegetation to fish and insects to lizards, and then eventually to man.[9]

What this all meant in practice is that other forms of life were classified, and even judged, according to their resemblance to men and women. Every human feature, such as living on land, having warm blood or walking on two legs, became an 'advance', an increase in status within the animal kingdom. In being separated from reptiles, amphibians were, in effect, 'demoted', but the ordering principle was not affected in the least. The fact that most amphibians spent the early parts of their lives in water, essentially as fish, and the later parts on land, essentially as 'lizards', seemed to confirm the hierarchical structure, since it showed a movement from a primitive to a more complex form of life.[10] 'Lizard' was less of a fixed category and more of a morphological pattern, which an animal might follow in varying degrees or at different stages in its life cycle.

With regard to everyday usage, the categories describing living things are fairly constant across cultural boundaries. The ethnozoologist Brent Berlin has maintained that the classification of living organisms is innate, and independent of either practical usefulness or symbolic significance. Some categories such as trees or birds have very distinct forms that make them seem to stand out from their surroundings.[11] But scientific nomenclatures have become, over the past few centuries, increasingly divorced from our intuitive perception. The word 'fish', which is still easily understandable in everyday conversation, no longer has any scientific meaning.[12]

Scientists no longer classify living things on the basis of a few characteristics, as they did from the eighteenth through the early twentieth centuries. They use databases that list scores

– even hundreds – of features, from which indexes of similarity are generated by computer. The favoured model for taxonomy is now cladistics, developed in the mid-twentieth century by the German entomologist Willi Hennig and popularized by Julian Huxley. Cladistics holds that classification of living things should follow biological evolution, which is diagrammed as a branching tree. The unit of classification is the 'clade', which consists of all organisms that share a common ancestor. The most empirically oriented cladists maintain that traditional categories such as genus and species are now anachronistic, since organisms can be identified simply and precisely in terms of a place on a 'cladogram', or evolutionary tree. Other zoologists believe that intuition, which plays an important role in traditional taxonomies, is fundamental to biology, perhaps playing a role comparable to that of empathy in medicine.

Books such as field guides or pet-owner manuals generally use taxonomies that are at least decades out of date. The authors are not necessarily ignorant of recent developments, but the older classifications are simpler and more intuitive. Writers on animals, except for a few of the most technical, are eclectic in their use of classifications, speaking in terms of 'species' or 'clades', depending on the context.

Today, the term 'lizard', like 'fish', is mostly part of 'folk taxonomy', since it does not occur in any scientific system of classification, and popular usage, in any case, does not always follow the lines of biological terminology. To avoid excessive confusion, popular books on animals endeavour to align the common and scientific terminologies, but these publications are not consistent with one another. The most restrictive position is to use the term 'lizard' only for members of the family Lacertidae, which are sometimes also referred to as 'true lizards'. These are small creatures that are especially common around the Mediterranean, and,

Sirene tiré de Barbot

Poisson armé d'une Corne
Aigüe tiré de Barbot

Poisson volant
tiré de Kolben

Dorade tiré de Kolben

Cheval marin
tiré de Frasier

Ston Brassem

Lyon de Mer
tiré de Kolben

Raie du Cap tiré
de Kolben

Cheval de Riviere nommé Vache marine au cap

Ventre de la Raie du Cap

with their slender, supple bodies, really do epitomize almost everything that the term 'lizard' suggests.

Many books state that lizards are all members of the order Squamata, as are snakes. Squamates are reptiles with scales, and the order includes over 9,000 identified species of at-times-baffling diversity. Amphisbaenians, which also belong to that order, look like snakes, but are anatomically closer to lizards, and they are at times informally placed in either category. To make things still more complicated, they move rather like worms. The word 'lizard', however, is also commonly applied to crocodilians and tuataras, as well as several other animals that do not belong to the Squamata at all.

In this book, I will designate the varieties of lizard using a combination of scientific and popular nomenclatures, but, all things being equal, I will prefer the common term. Colloquial terminologies often sound more vivid, and have the advantage of placing an animal more clearly in the worlds of both nature and human society. Popular nomenclatures generally develop organically over decades or centuries, and help us to maintain continuity with the past. Scientific nomenclatures are, in some respects, more artificial, since they are generally fixed by one person or by a team. They are neither innate nor socially constructed so much as mandated by authority. Common names may not always be used in a uniform way, but neither are scientific ones, which are constantly disputed in esoteric debates.

Traditional names of animals, by a process known as 'phon-aesthesia', even metaphorically suggest qualities such as the size, shape and motion of a creature through their sound.[13] The resonant word 'lizard' has a rhythmic pattern that calls to mind a small, lithe, rapidly moving creature. Lizards have a primeval quality that transcends their taxonomic status. They blend into many environments, from rocky coasts to deserts and rainforests. Because of this adaptability, they evoke many analogies and metaphors. Their fluid motion can make us think of water, while their curvilinear forms suggest vegetation. Their stillness suggests death, while their explosive movement is like resurrection.

I have chosen to risk forgoing some empirical precision, and regard the word 'lizard' primarily as designating a sort of pattern, a form that is directly inherited but may perhaps also be attained through convergence. My focus will be largely on squamates, apart from snakes, but nothing that even looks 'like a lizard', from a dinosaur to a space alien, will be entirely outside the notice of this book.

2 The Diversity of Lizards

At noon in the desert a panting lizard
waited for history . . .
William E. Stafford, 'At the Bomb Testing Site'

Zoologists count about 6,000 species of lizard, even excluding crocodilians – far more than all other species of reptiles combined. This multiplicity of varieties parallels that of human cultures. While humans and lizards share a remarkable degree of adaptability, they achieve this in sharply contrasting ways. Humans change their environments, while lizards settle into very specific, specialized niches. Despite being similar to one another in their basic morphology, lizards have a dazzling range of colours, textures and physical ornaments. They have adjusted to new environmental conditions by acquiring different means of locomotion, diets, sizes, habits, senses, patterns of sleep and ways of foraging for food. Many highly distinctive species are confined to single islands or similarly restricted locations. By specializing, lizards minimize competition with other creatures, thereby enhancing rather than threatening their ecosystem, and so perhaps lizards have something to teach us about living in harmony with the environment.

Lizards, like other animals, exist for us on three levels: common sense, science and creative imagination. To combine these three is a never-ending negotiation, but with lizards it is especially difficult. Outside very warm climates, they are not often seen. The places they prefer are not usually congenial to human beings. Their habitats may be either too wet, like soil under a rotting log in

a forest, or too dry, like a burrow in the desert. Their often obscure locations, while they keep lizards from human awareness, also endow the creatures with mystery. Without attempting to be exhaustive, this chapter will look at some lizards of the world, as well as at a few of their most dramatic characteristics.

A gargoyle gecko, indigenous to New Caledonia. Note how the gecko is washing its eyes with its tongue.

Geckos are indigenous to every continent except Antarctica, which suggests that their lineage was in place before the great land masses drifted apart, and they may be close to the original variety from which all other lizards evolved. They have so many unique adaptations that even seasoned herpetologists can feel baffled by them. Eric R. Pianka and Laurie J. Vitt write:

Windshield-wiper tongues, adhesive toe and tail pads, skin that feels like rubber, lightning-speed color change, fixed small clutch size, and chirps in the night all provide clues to the many directions gekkotan evolution has taken. Indeed, geckoes have experimented with evolution in a nearly surreal fashion.[1]

Geckos have the capacity to cling to, and move across, vertical surfaces, or even walk upside down, which mystified scientists for decades. Researchers looked for some sort of glue or for suction cups, but there was no sign of either. It took an electron microscope for scientists, in the late 1960s, finally to figure out how the adhesion was accomplished. The toe pads (setae) of geckos are covered with microscopic hairs, each of which divides into about twenty filaments equipped with hooks. The fasteners are so tiny that they can make use of intermolecular forces, latching on to minute irregularities in surfaces, even when these appear very smooth. The pads cling so tightly to a surface that geckos cannot simply raise their feet in a single movement, but must pry them away, starting at the edges. Human beings have not managed to create anything synthetic that remotely approaches the efficiency of setae on gecko feet, but, in trying to duplicate this, researchers created Velcro, which is relatively crude and adheres only to specifically designed materials, but operates on a similar principle.

Also remarkable are the gecko's eyes, which, in most species, do not close. The pupils are generally round during the night, when most geckos are foraging for insects, but diminish to a vertical slit during the day. This gives them a steady, neotenous gaze, which can suggest human infants or space aliens. Geckos clean their eyes by licking them with their tongues. They may even be the origin of the 'little green men' from outer space, from popular culture of the middle to late twentieth century.

Appealing as they appear, geckos are not very easy to keep as pets, since most of them can easily scale the glass walls of a terrarium and even escape across the ceiling. One gecko that is especially popular as a companion animal is the small leopard gecko, indigenous to the Central Asian plains, which lacks toe pads and setae, and has only small claws instead. It may be named for having yellow skin with dark, brown spots, but the resemblance to a leopard does not end there. Unlike most geckos, it can raise itself on comparatively straight legs well above the ground. Like a leopard, it hunts its prey, which is insects, relying largely on darkness and stealth.

Unlike other varieties of lizard, geckos are pretty consistent in appearance, though there are a few outliers among them. The Namib desert gecko of southwest Africa has developed webs on its feet, enabling it to glide across desert sand, almost as though it were swimming in water. Its internal organs are visible through its delicate skin, and its eyes, even for a gecko, are unusually large in proportion to its body. This gives it an otherworldly appearance, which suggests a spectral visitor.

The camouflage used by geckos in the forests of Madagascar illustrates the extremes of specialization of which lizards are capable. The lined leaf-tailed gecko has skin the colour and texture of peeling bark, and camouflages itself almost perfectly by lying vertically, head downwards, on the stem of a tree. The mossy leaf-tailed gecko disguises itself as a mass of lichens and moss. Their smaller relative, the fantastic leaf-tailed gecko, is very easily mistaken for a spray of autumn foliage.

In recent times, the Geico Gecko, a cartoon reptile with a Cockney accent, has become perhaps the most visible animal mascot in American advertising. He walks upright like a human being and uses his forelegs as arms, but never eats insects or climbs walls. His huge eyes help to evoke empathy, befitting a salesman for accident insurance, while he softens the gravity of his subject through humour. Geckos are the only lizards with

Namib desert gecko. Note the rounded prints in the sand that are left by its webbed feet.

The silhouette of a gecko against a leaf. Note the prominent toe pads.

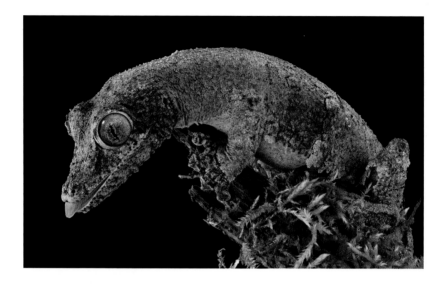

vocal cords, and their name probably comes from an attempt to transcribe the calls that some of these creatures make throughout the night. Geico initially used a gecko in advertising primarily for puns on, and little jokes about, the company name, but the firm and the public gradually became very fond of the image of the gecko as well.

Female mossy leaf-tailed gecko of Madagascar camouflaged as a branch covered with moss and lichens.

Lizards gradually differentiated as the supercontinent of Pangaea broke apart, a process that began about 200 million years ago and was completed about 135 million years later. The most closely related families include iguanids in Latin America; agamids in Africa, Europe, Asia and Australia; and anoles in North America. Iguanas are the most colourful and dramatic of lizards. Their flamboyant hues and crests can suggest, rather anthropomorphically, a barbaric sort of splendour. They show a high degree of sexual dimorphism, and the most elaborate ornamentation, as with most birds, is confined to the males, which need to impress the ladies. In many species, the colours of the males become a lot brighter in hue during mating season.

When lizards have been used in Hollywood B-movies as stand-ins for dinosaurs, dragons or space aliens, they are almost always iguanids. These lizards also do 'push-ups' for several reasons, including to impress prospective mates and scare away rivals. The depth, pacing and sequence of the head bobs vary with the species, gender and situation of the lizards, and constitute a form of communication, perhaps not entirely unlike Morse code. The bobbing head can look to us like a gesture of assent, a disconcertingly human sign from a creature that, in so many ways, seems very alien.

The best known of these lizards is the green iguana, a native of Mexico and Latin America, which is a popular pet in the United

While features such as the crest may seem exotic, the partially closed eye and posture of this green iguana suggest an almost human sort of deliberation.

States, but is capable of growing to a length of 2 m (7 ft). These lizards have impressive rows of spines running down their backs, and dewlaps, or throat pouches. Another well-known iguana is the green basilisk lizard, also known as the Jesus Christ lizard, found in Central and South American rainforests. The male has a very high crest running from its head down its back and about half the length of its tail. The basilisk lizard is mostly arboreal, but always lives close to a body of water, and plunges into it when

startled. It can run on its two hind legs over rivers, vigorously pumping its forelegs and swinging its tail to maintain balance.

Many iguanids are proficient swimmers and some of them have even found their way to Pacific islands, where, in the absence of trees, they have learned to live on low-lying plants such as succulents. An iguanid found only on the Galápagos Islands, the marine iguana, feeds entirely on seaweed, and is one of extremely few primarily aquatic lizards in the world. It has a prominent dorsal crest of spines and partially webbed feet. Rather like a seal, it spends its time, when not foraging for food, sunning itself on rocks.

Agamids are a related lizard family found in Africa, Asia and Australia, and they have adapted to their environment in ways that seem even more surreal. Their tribe is full of the oddities, anomalies and paradoxes that constantly fascinated the Victorians and continue to intrigue us today. One unusual lizard is the frilled lizard of Australia, which spreads out a large ruffle of skin around its head to frighten predators by increasing its size, and then runs on its two forelegs to find shelter by scaling a tree. Another is the flying dragon, found in Southeast Asia, which spreads out large folds of skin attached to mobile ribs on each side of its body, enabling it to glide from one tree to another.

Perhaps the most dramatic agamid of all is the Australian thorny dragon, also known as the Moloch lizard, which is covered with spikes. In a parched environment, it can use the cleavages in its armour to direct dew into its mouth. When threatened by predators, it will bury its head in the sand and raise its tail, so that it looks like a desert plant. It has a round, spiked appendage on the back of its neck, which serves as a 'false head' to distract potential predators. Despite its name, which recalls the Carthaginian deity to whom human children were allegedly sacrificed, the thorny devil eats only ants.

Plumed basilisk lizard resting on a branch. If there is any disturbance in the adjacent forest canopy, this lizard will drop down and then run along the surface of the water.

Marine iguana sunning itself on Fernandina Island in the Galápagos.

Frilled lizard, from an 18th-century book of natural history.

'Flying Dragon' by William Daniell, illustration to *Oriental Scenery* (1807). This agama lizard can soar half the length of a football field, with minimal loss of altitude, and then land gracefully.

The thorny dragon, also known as the Moloch lizard, indigenous to Western Australia. The body of this lizard mirrors the colours and textures of the rough, rocky soil. The raised tail, which sways as the lizard walks along, resembles a succulent plant in the wind.

The agamid most beloved as a pet is probably the bearded dragon, several varieties of which are found in Australia. It is distinguished by rows or clusters of spiked scales found on its throat. Its natural habitat is scrublands and deserts, where it has developed a toughness that now makes it easy to keep in captivity. It has a flattened body, with spikes along the edges of its stomach. Part of its popularity is probably due to a wide mouth, which seems to open in a big smile. Its skin is generally a golden tone, but both its colour changes and its body language seem very expressive.

The Carolina anoles, indigenous to the American Southeast and the Caribbean, bring together many of the most dramatic features of many lizard species. Like geckos, they have toe pads with setae, which enable them to climb trees or walls easily. They are also sometimes known, a bit deceptively, as 'the American chameleon', since they can take on many hues of brown and green. But the relatively unique feature by which these lizards are known is their especially large dewlaps. Those of the males are bright red or yellow. They flick these pouches down and up, creating sudden flashes of colour to signal their presence to females, while hopefully not drawing much attention from animals that prey on them. The dewlaps of the females are far smaller and a modest but attractive white.

Probably the strangest lizard of all is the chameleon, which is most common on the island of Madagascar, but is also found throughout much of Africa, South Asia and parts of Europe. Chameleons have long, prehensile tails that help them cling to trees. The five appendages on their feet are fused into two groups, three on one side and two on the other, which face in opposing directions and help them to cling tightly to branches. They also expand and compress their bodies, shifting their centres of gravity and maintaining balance. This enables them to climb at a slow but very steady gait, though they are awkward on the ground.

A panther chameleon, native to Madagascar. Note the prehensile tail, the turret-like eye and how the body is compressed as it waits in stillness for an insect.

Carolina anole lizard.

An Australian bearded dragon clings to a girl's sleeve at the reptile exposition at the Westchester County Center, New York.

Komodo dragon.

They do not need, or have reason, to move very much, however, since they are consummate ambush predators. A chameleon will stay entirely still for an incredibly long time, and then, in less than a tenth of a second, shoot out its tongue at an insect with amazing accuracy. The tongue can expand to over two and a half times the chameleon's body length. It adheres to the prey using a combination of moisture and suction, and then reels the insect back into the chameleon's mouth.

But what gives the chameleon an especially otherworldly appearance is its eyes, which rotate and focus separately, enabling the creature to see in two directions at once, as well as to see everything within an arc of almost 360 degrees. Only when the chameleon is stalking an insect do both eyes focus in a single direction, giving it stereoscopic vision to judge the distance of its prey.

Since we human beings orient ourselves so much by sight, which we think of as a single plane, it is especially difficult to imagine the world of a chameleon. Each eye can appear as a separate centre of consciousness, occupying what is otherwise a single creature. Like Faust in Goethe's famous poem, the chameleon seems to have 'two souls'.

Members of the family Varanidae evoke ambivalence, since they are at once the most frightening of lizards and the most like human beings. Most other lizards are insectivores, but varanids will eat other lizards, eggs, birds and mammals. They hunt by extending their long, forked tongues, which are used not for ingestion but to detect chemical traces of possible prey.

At the same time, these lizards are renowned for their intelligence and adaptability. In an odd instance of convergence, varanids have developed a neurophysiology that is very similar to that of mammals.[2] They will meet the gaze of a human being in a disconcerting way that appears to hover between threat and

A baby panther chameleon shooting out its tongue to catch a cricket.

A somewhat fanciful monitor lizard, from *Locupletissimi rerum naturalium* by Albertus Seba (*c.* 1734). The artist seems to have sensed the capacity of these lizards for empathy, and the eye seems almost human.

affection. In zoos, they often develop personal relationships with their attendants, who say they like to be scratched and petted.

The largest and most fearsome of these lizards is the Komodo dragon, which is found only on Komodo and a few other islands off the coast of Indonesia. It was discovered in 1910, when a Dutch pilot was forced to land there unexpectedly and, on seeing such huge lizards, initially thought he had discovered a refuge of dinosaurs. These lizards grow to up to 3 m (10 ft) in length, eat mostly large prey such as deer and may even attack human beings. Their mode of hunting seems to entail a nearly 'human' combination of intelligence and cruelty. They will wound a deer with a bite and then, instead of fighting it, withdraw until their prey collapses from a combination of toxins in the lizard's saliva and loss of blood, after which they will devour it.

Juvenile Komodo dragons can climb trees, an ability that they lose later in life. It is necessary for the survival of the species that young Komodo dragons have this ability and that older ones not retain it, because the adult Komodo dragons regularly eat the juveniles, which have no other means of escape. Unenlightened as such a response may seem, it is hard to think of this species without a touch of dread. But, though relentless predators, Komodo dragons are not incapable of empathy. They often form lasting mated pairs, and recognize individual keepers when in captivity.

Reptiles in the family Lacertidae epitomize everything we understand by the term 'lizard' – in fact, they are sometimes referred to as 'true lizards'. They are very slender and relatively small, with very flexible bodies, long tails and a wide variety of patterns and colours, but they lack the physical ornamentation of iguanas and many other lizards. Their status as a sort of paradigm is, however, in part because they are common around the Mediterranean, where the foundations of zoology were established by Aristotle, Galen and others. Wall lizards in that region are constantly scampering over rocks and walls, and artists often depict them among the ruins of Greek and Roman temples.

Lacertids lie so still that people often mistake them for corpses, but then hurry away so quickly that they almost appear to vanish by magic when they have been startled or enticed by insect prey. These lizards are also common in Africa, and feral populations, consisting mostly of abandoned pets, are establishing themselves throughout much of the world.

The closest biological relatives of lacertids in the Americas and the West Indies are lizards of the family Teiidae, such as whiptails and tegus, which have similar streamlined physiques and occupy the same biological niche. Teiids are distinguished from lacertids mostly in having solid teeth, which are fastened to their jawbones.

Illustration to Comte de Buffon's *Histoire naturelle*, probably showing a Latin American whiptail lizard, which he simply described as 'dragon' (1799). He thought it resembled a crocodile, but added that the creature was distinguished by its tongue, 'which it stretches out in a frightening manner'.

Gymnophalamids are essentially miniature teiids, and live mostly under the leaves at the base of trees in the rainforests of Central and South America. Most have transparent eyelids, which allow them to see even when their eyes are closed, but, in contrast to those of geckos, their lids are also moveable. They are exceptionally diverse, and many species are specific to a small area of the forest floor.

'Elegant Ophiops', *c.* 1890. Wall lizards have conventionally been shown climbing the walls and pillars of Graeco-Roman temples.

Yet another major family of lizards is Scincidae, which generally have reduced limbs, fairly round torsos and very long tails, often making them resemble snakes. Most of them create homes by burrowing, though a few are aquatic or arboreal. Of all lizards, skinks are the most widely dispersed, and have the greatest variety of social behaviour. Some form monogamous pairs, and a few even care for their young, behaviours once thought exclusive to the so-called 'higher' animals such as mammals.

Among the most iconic is the shingleback skink, a large, viviparous, Australian lizard with heavy scales and a stubby tail. Male and female shingleback skinks mate, and then separate, after which the female gives birth to her offspring three to five months later. The next spring, the mother and father find one another by means of pheromones and renew their partnership, and they may continue to do that every year for their entire lifetimes of up to two decades or more. If one of the mated partners dies in the presence of the other, the remaining shingleback will delicately lick the body of its mate. This is one of those behaviours found in animals, like the 'funerals' held by crows or the bones revisited by

A mated pair of shingleback skinks. We may be subject to anthropomorphic illusion, but it is hard to look at the faces of these skinks without sensing a glimmer of romance.

A five-lined skink guarding its eggs in Ontario, Canada.

elephants, that seems uncannily suggestive of a human wake, and its interpretation may always be poised between science and folklore. But, contrary to what one might anticipate, the bond between these reptilian lovers has nothing to do with parental care, since the mother abandons her young as soon as they are born. The large, fierce, prehensile-tailed skink of the Solomon Islands, however, uses its powerful limbs and long claws to protect its young from boas, rats and raptors during their first year of life. The long, slender, female, five-lined skink of North America lays eggs and winds her body around them – not to incubate the eggs but to provide protection.

The family Helodermatidae consists of venomous lizards, and is confined to North America, the best-known representative being the Gila monster of the American Southwest and the beaded lizard of Mexico and Guatemala. They have relatively stocky

Gila monster.
The hunched
pose and steady
gaze of this lizard
suggest a relentless
predator, though
it is probably only
stalking insects.

builds, and are about 56 cm (22 in.) in length, with large, circular
scales, and spend most of their time in burrows. They move with
heavy, ponderous steps, which contrasts with the quickness of
lacertids. Too slow to hunt very well, they largely survive on eggs,
carrion, insects and small birds or mammals. In times of drought,
they can lie dormant beneath the surface of the earth for months,
living off the fat stored in their tails, and then startle people by
suddenly emerging, where their presence had not been suspected,
after rain.

Lizards of the family Phrynosomatidae also tend to thrive in
deserts, and they are widespread through much of Central and
North America. The best known of these is the short-horned
lizard, which is the mascot of many schools and an unofficial
symbol of Texas. Because of its squat, rounded body, it has also
been known, a bit erroneously, as the 'horny toad'. It has horns
on its head and several spikes on its scales. This rough texture,

together with its shades of reddish brown, enable the Texas short-horned lizard to blend in almost perfectly with the rocky soil of the desert. It is an ambush predator, which lives exclusively on ants that it catches by shooting out its tongue. It can distract its predators by squirting blood from its eyes, which can appeal to both the Amerindian practice of sacrifice and the Christian veneration of martyrdom. Among the Mexicans, it is called *torito de la Virgen* or 'the Virgin's little bull'.

Some people do not count crocodilians as lizards, but the tribe of lizards would seem diminished without them. These include crocodiles, alligators, caimans and gharials. They are found in coastal areas and some rivers in Africa, Asia and the Americas, and are the subject of a vast, and highly varied, amount of lore, from the ancient Egyptians to the Maya. They are huge, with crocodiles and alligators growing to well over 6 m (20 ft) in length, and their terrifying aspect is accentuated by large and highly visible teeth. Though supposedly lowly creatures, they will feed on large mammals such as wildebeests or monkeys, and even on men, women or children. This often gives them an ambiguous status, which hovers between diabolic and godly, in myths and legends.

Short-horned toad from Mexico, from Leopold Fitzinger, *Bilder-Atlas zur wissenschaflichen populären Naturgeschichte der Wirbelthiere* (1867).

Fig. 21 a.

A TEXAS HORNED TOAD SMOKING A CIGARETTE——T18

Postcard from the early 1950s showing a Texas short-horned toad smoking a cigarette. The popularity of these lizards has been a mixed blessing, since people sometimes want to 'humanize' them a bit too much.

Finally, there is the tuatara, which is also not always considered a 'lizard', yet, in many ways, seems to epitomize the primeval qualities that word suggests. Researchers often consider the tuatara a 'living fossil', seemingly little changed for more than 200 million years, and it has a 'primitive' appearance, with very rough, scaly skin and a crest of spines running down its back. It is easy to imagine the tuatara, along with crocodiles, mingling with dinosaurs. Although the degree to which the species has remained constant over eons is disputed, biologists look to the tuatara for clues about the evolution of lizards in general, especially iguanids, which they most resemble. For the past two centuries or so, tuataras have been confined to a handful of islands off the coast of New Zealand, though they are now being reintroduced to the mainland with some success. Tuataras are reportedly especially susceptible to music, and people can entice them out of their burrows by singing or playing instruments.[3]

Until recently, social critics could blame war, violent crime or terrorism on the 'lizard brain'. The theory of the triune brain held that evolution of the brain in vertebrates has been by accretion, and that the human brain is divided into three successive layers that accumulated over eons. First is the reptilian complex, also known as the 'lizard brain', which is responsible for aggression, ritualized displays, territorial behaviour and social hierarchies. The second is the limbic system, also known as the 'palaeomammalian complex', which is responsible for emotions, parenting and more complex social interactions. Finally, there is the neocortex, which is the site of abstract thinking, intuition and morality. According to this theory, each of the three layers continues to operate with some autonomy, together generating complex behaviour. This idea had been anticipated by Sigmund Freud, fully articulated by Paul McClean in the early 1960s and then publicized by Carl Sagan in his best-seller *The Dragons of Eden* of 1977.[4]

It followed that – mentally at least – lizards and other reptiles were essentially primitive human beings, which had only the first of the human brain's three layers. Reptiles were, therefore, intellectually little changed since diverging from us in evolution around 280 million years ago. The theory entered popular culture, producing a number of manuals on how to negotiate with, or bypass, the more primeval layers of one's mind. This concept is now discredited for many reasons. It fails to explain the vast variation of abilities that zoologists have found in virtually all animals and even in plants. Birds such as New Caledonian crows are able to make complex tools, and African grey parrots have remarkable linguistic capacities. Birds, like some fish and reptiles, care for their young, despite lacking a neocortex. The quality known as

A somewhat fanciful picture of an alligator from a book of natural history, late 18th century. The artist plainly thought of this creature as a giant lizard, since he gave it a very long tail and lithe body. Note the similarity to Tyrannosaurus rex.

'intelligence' – insofar as it is meaningful at all – turns out to be far more evenly divided among animals than researchers had once believed.

Cognitive psychology has been making remarkable discoveries about a vast array of animals, from dogs to ravens to octopuses, but lizards have – at least until recently – been comparatively neglected. That is starting to change. Experiments by Manuel S. Leal of Duke University recently showed that anoles, arboreal lizards found in parts of the southeastern United States and the Caribbean, showed far greater adaptability than was expected. Leal placed a tasty larva in a hole covered by a cap. The anoles normally pounce on prey from above, but that was not an option in the experiment's scenario. Out of six lizards, two gave up on obtaining the treat, but two others picked up the cap with their mouths from the side to remove it. Another pair pried off the cap using their noses. Experiments by John Phillips at the San Diego Zoo suggest that monitor lizards can count to six. The lizards were conditioned to expect up to six snails in a chamber,

Bryan Talbot, illustration to the graphic novel *Grandville Noël* (2014). Tiberius König, the 'Napoleon of Crime', is a satiric embodiment of the proverbial 'lizard brain'.

and then, when one was removed, they searched for the missing bit of food.[5] But it is not appropriate to measure the abilities of lizards solely by criteria that were developed for people, dogs or chimpanzees, and they have many capacities that no mammals can match.

One of the features that can make iguanids and tuataras seem uncanny is the presence of a vestigial third, or parietal, eye on the top of the head. This is generally clearly visible in juveniles, though later in life it is obscured by skin and scales. The parietal eye does not see with sufficient clarity for the lizard to distinguish objects, but does perhaps see enough to distinguish between daylight and darkness. It probably plays a role in thermoregulation, by helping to control exposure to the sun.

The parietal eye has a remarkable resemblance to the third eye found in many representations of Asian deities. The organ is connected with the pineal gland, also known as the 'pineal eye', which is found in most vertebrates and seems to have a role in the hormonal regulation of circadian rhythms. Descartes believed that the pineal gland was the seat of the soul, and many traditions, both oriental and occidental, associate it with higher consciousness.

The third eye is especially noteworthy in pictures or sculptures of the meditating Buddha, since the practice of sitting

A tuatara. The rough spines and skin contribute to the primordial appearance of this creature. In this photograph, the parietal eye is just barely visible at the top of the head.

Illustration showing a whiptail lizard, from *Locupletissimi rerum naturalium* by Albertus Seba (*c.* 1734). When a lizard casts off part of its tail to escape a predator, a double tail sometimes grows in place of the original one, as in this illustration.

entirely still is also shared with lizards. The motif is a very ancient one, and it is impossible to trace whether it was originally inspired by the parietal eye. However that may be, it suggests the ability to see a world of spirits.

Lizards from several families share a remarkable ability to break off their tails, an ability known as autotomy, which is also found in many salamanders, some tuataras and a few snakes. The tail of a lacertid or other lizard still appears fully alive after it has been discarded, distracting a pursuing predator while the lizard gets away. A new tail immediately starts to grow, though its markings may be different from the original one. If the predator does not devour the tail, the lizard may return and eat it. Manuals often advise pet owners to handle these lizards with special care, since, if the animals are stressed, the tail could snap off in a person's hand, something that might not do a great deal of damage to the lizard but could be very disconcerting to the human.

Several arachnids, most famously the daddy longlegs, will also break off a limb as an offering to a pursuing predator. The analogy that comes most readily to mind, however, is with plants, which are less centrally organized than animals and can readily dispense with leaves or fruits, which then regrow in about a year. According to classical anthropologist Walter Burkert, this offering of a tail or other body part has many analogues in human society, from human sacrifice to scapegoating and martyrdom. The offering of a finger to a deity is especially widespread in cultures around the world. When the future of the deities appeared threatened, the Norse god Odin plucked out an eye and tossed it into a stream, in exchange for prophetic wisdom. In all of these cases, a part – of the individual body or of the larger community – is given up to save the rest.[6] Unassuming as many lizards appear, their example may have had an important influence on the very foundations of human civilization. In general, lacertids and their close relatives have many characteristics that may evoke ancestral memories of a remote time when human beings were closer to the animal kingdom and in constant danger of becoming prey.

Another characteristic of these lizards, which can seem almost paranormal, is parthenogenesis, in which a female organism can

Green lizard with two tails.

give birth without first being fertilized by a male. This ability is found in several lacertids, such as many species of Caucasian rock lizards, as well as in a few teiids such as the New Mexican whiptail, and occasionally even among Komodo dragons. Parthenogenesis at times occurs after two closely related yet distinct varieties of lizard mate. Offspring of two mammals that are related yet belong to different species, such as the mule produced by a jack (male donkey) and a mare (female horse), are usually sterile. When two species of lacertids mate, by contrast, the offspring can be very fertile, but their mode of reproduction is no longer sexual. The entire population is female, and their numbers grow very quickly. Since, however, all are genetically identical, this new variety has hardly any ability to adapt to changing conditions, and may be easily wiped out by a new disease or a change in climate.

Parthenogenesis is also common among microorganisms and plants, and is found in some insects, such as aphids, as well as some arachnids, such as scorpions. According to legends, a great number of cultural and religious figures had virgin births, including Zoroaster, Moses, Jesus, Mithra and Muhammad. In the second creation story in the Bible, Adam, though male, gives birth to Eve, assisted by God. There are no verified accounts of parthenogenesis occurring spontaneously in human beings, though the stories of this may have helped to inspire reproductive technologies such as surrogate pregnancy. Parthenogenesis generates a special fascination in lizards, since they usually seem to be at least a bit closer to being 'human' than other living things that have this ability.

Changes of skin colouration are most intimately associated with chameleons, but are also found in other lizards such as geckos and skinks. To a very limited extent, human beings share the ability of chameleons and other lizards to communicate through changes in colour. We can 'turn red' through embarrassment or anger, and we can also 'feel blue'. But comparing our ability at this with that of a chameleon is likely to make us 'green with envy'.

Lizards accomplish their changes of colour by stretching and contracting two superimposed layers of skin, to expose different pigments. Recent research indicates that, in chameleons at least, the second layer of skin contains microscopic crystals, which reflect and absorb different wavelengths of light according to their orientation.[7] The reasons for the change are even more mysterious than the mechanism. These include changes of mood, camouflage and sexual readiness.

The colours also serve thermoregulation by growing darker to absorb more sunlight when the temperature becomes too low, and then turning brighter to reflect more sun when it is warmer. With chameleons, which can also change their shape to a considerable extent, the alterations of hue could even work in concert with a variable morphology. The shifting colours, in summary, are a sort of language with which lizards communicate both with one another and with their environment, in ways that we can barely begin to understand.

The fact that the colour of chameleons and other lizards responds so readily to changes in light raises the interesting question of whether a lizard can legitimately be said to 'see' with its skin, a question that could also be asked in relation to octopuses, which change colour in response to similar conditions, and their relatives. The question might also be raised with regard to plants, which also respond to the light, if not quite so instantaneously. Leaves turn to the light, and morning glories open with the morning sun.

This phenomenon raises interesting philosophical questions about the nature of perception and consciousness. If these lizards do not have an intense sense of the self as something apart from the external world, they may not experience the same gap between perception and reaction. For them, in a very intimate way, one could truly say that 'seeing is believing'.

Viewed anthropomorphically, the faces of lizards often suggest a combination of fierceness and melancholy, which can be very appealing. The body language of lizards is expressive, yet not so easy to translate into human terms. We human beings can communicate with enormous subtlety, not only through language, but by such means as a gaze or a tone of voice. Lizards use other means entirely. What lizards impart, at least to us, is not primarily emotion, but closer to a sort of wisdom. Lizards are enchanting without ceasing to be ordinary, a bit like the charmed lamps or twigs of fairy tales.

Without extensive study, lizards are very difficult to categorize, picture or describe, and confusing the characteristics of different species will be all but inevitable. All of the intricate techniques of camouflage, feints and secret signals that lizards have worked out in collaboration with Mother Nature – for such purposes as intimidating predators, concealing themselves from prey and impressing potential mates – can fool human observers too. Before Linnaeus and others began the scientific classification of living things, chameleons of a single species changing colour or modifying their form could easily have been mistaken for entirely different varieties. It would have been easy for a human observer to mistake the young Komodo dragons, ensconced in trees, and old Komodo dragons, on the ground, for different varieties of lizard, related perhaps only as predator and prey. The enormous diversity of lizards can bewilder the intellect and inspire the imagination, but human creativity enhances even this variety, to create an even vaster range of serpents and dragons.

Human beings have never entered into a partnership with any variety of lizard in the way that we have with dogs, bees, sheep, cats, silkworms, horses, pigs, cattle and many other animals. It might not be appropriate to call them 'companion species', but that does not mean that lizards have not had a profound influence on human culture. The range and vividness of our imaginations is a defining characteristic of human beings, and lizards have perhaps a unique ability to stimulate our fantasies.

3 Lizards and Dragons

But it is one thing to read about dragons and another to meet them.
Ursula K. Le Guin

People are eating in a restaurant when an enormous shadow, rather like a dragon, passes above them. Tourists gaze up in amazement to see a gecko crawling across a fluorescent light, probably in hope that some delicious insects will be attracted to the glow. The regulars simply continue eating or talking, for this is a familiar occurrence. It takes place in warm locales, from Spain to Thailand, where these lizards are common.

In human culture as well, the modest lizard casts an enormous shadow. At times, it seems as though lizards are strangely absent from many great myths in which other animals such as snakes, wolves and bees have such prominent roles. With lizards, however, nature has adopted a strategy that, in ways, seems oddly human – taking a basic form and then adding virtually endless variations and embellishments. Human culture continues that process, making lizards into a vast range of magical dragons.

The anthropologist Gregory Forth has examined the grouping of lizards among the Nage, a people of eastern Indonesia. They distinguish five different kinds of lizard, each of which is identified with very distinctive religious and social properties. The house gecko, which is so tiny that it can easily fit into the palm of a person's hand, foretells the future with chirps, and may sometimes be a relative visiting from the world beyond. The flying dragon can draw lightning from the sky, and then escape by gliding

down from a tree. The many-lined skink mates with domestic sows. The tokay gecko, which is relatively large and brilliantly coloured, is often used in medicines. The water monitor, which can grow to over 1.8 m (6 ft) in length, is notoriously deceptive, and reportedly likes to fool people by leaving tracks facing backwards. Among the Nage, 'lizard' is a 'covert taxon'. These creatures are implicitly associated, yet there is no indigenous word for 'lizard' in the Nage language. They elude classification in terms of Nage mythology, since, unlike almost all other creatures, they are associated neither with earth spirits nor with witches.[1]

While it is always hard to generalize about human societies, the same pattern seems applicable to lizards in other cultures as well. There are plenty of folk tales about a generic snake, rabbit or turtle, but very few about a lizard, in which the approximate variety is neither specified nor clear from the context. Cultures may

Light in Playa Maderas, Nicaragua. A gecko is chasing insects on the surface of a paper lantern, creating a silhouette and casting shadows.

The house gecko in the hands of a child. This diminutive creature, which often enters human homes, is native to southern Indonesia and parts of northern Australia. They are sometimes regarded as deceased relatives, returning from the world beyond.

assign specific symbolic meanings to various species of lizard, but the category itself is too diverse for any unitary symbolism. Suppose we try to sum up all the five kinds of lizards distinguished by the Nage, and perhaps some others in addition, in a concept or – better still – an image. You would have a figure of great complexity and ambivalence.

That figure, of course, is a dragon, a creature that seems to appear in almost every human culture. Most fantastic creatures of mythology and folklore either have a single prototype in nature or else are composites of two or three. The unicorn is generally a horse or goat with the horn of a narwhal; the griffin usually has the body of a lion but the head and claws of an eagle; and the mermaid is a woman with the tail of a fish. The dragon, by contrast, may incorporate features of countless animals, from bats to peacocks, yet generally does this so harmoniously that the borrowing may not be immediately apparent. No other creature of the imagination has such a vast range of features and symbolic meanings, yet remains easily recognizable. Many lizards have the word 'dragon' in their names. There are water, bearded, flying, Komodo, mountain, thorny and sailfin 'dragons', to mention only a few varieties. Under the almost endless ornaments, the basic form of the dragon is a lizard.

The Asian, or Chinese, dragon is perhaps the most widely depicted mythological animal in the world today. Representations of this creature go back to very remote times, and have changed

An 18th-century illustration from a book of natural history showing a flying dragon descending from a tree. Its tail flashing across the sky is suggestive of lightning.

surprisingly little since the Shang dynasty (1600–1046 BCE). It has an elongated body with four short legs, an extended tail and a pair of horns. It takes on very dynamic poses, rhythmically twisting and turning its body. The dragon traditionally holds or pursues a pearl, which might represent the moon or simply wisdom, but which is very suggestive of an egg and might, at one time, have been one. In the Chou dynasty (1046–256 BCE), a yellow dragon with five claws became the symbol of the Chinese emperor, and it was traditionally paired with the Feng Huang, or 'Chinese phoenix', which represents the empress.

The Chinese dragon is a shape-changer that can make itself smaller than a caterpillar or so large that its shadow darkens the sky. It can change colour, and has a different hue for every season.

Dragon dance to celebrate the Asian New Year, Manhattan's Chinatown, 2011.

Dish showing a dragon, Ming Dynasty, China. This dragon has five claws, which makes it the symbol of the Emperor. To paint such a creature without royal permission was punishable by death.

Chinese dragon embroidered with silk, *c.* 19th century. To maintain balance, lizards generally involve their entire bodies in every motion, which creates a graceful dance. Similarly, the Asian dragon is almost never shown in a stationary pose, but is always bending and turning.

A blue dragon of the East rules in spring; a yellow or red dragon of the South in summer; a white dragon of the West in autumn; and a black dragon of the North in winter. The dragon also combines the elements. The kingdom of the dragon is often beneath the surface of the water, and the dragon brings rain, yet it is often depicted running or flying. Mist almost always surrounds the dragon, and flames shoot out from its moving limbs.

According to a famous description attributed to Confucian scholar Wang Fu in the Han dynasty (206 BCE–220 CE), the dragon has attributes of nine animals: the horns of a stag, head of a camel, eyes of a hare, neck of a snake, stomach of a mussel, scales of a carp, claws of an eagle, paws of a tiger and ears of an ox.[2] In the words of anthropologist Roel Sterckx, the dragon 'epitomized the image of the sacred animal as an embodiment of change' and 'represented all animals in one without losing its original shape'.[3]

The lizard is not among the nine animals that, according to Wang Fu, contribute to the Chinese dragon. One feature found in Chinese depictions of dragons – a characteristic that Wang Fu did not mention – is a crest reaching from the head, down the back and all the way to the end of the tail. This is characteristic of many lizards and their close relatives, including lacertids, agamids, chameleons and tuataras. So why didn't Wang Fu add as a tenth attribute of the dragon the 'dorsal crest of a lizard'? Perhaps he simply thought of the dragon as essentially a lizard and, in consequence, took that for granted. The dragon certainly has the form of one, with the combination of scales, claws, short legs, a long tail and, above all, an extremely lithe, flexible body.

The size and power of the crocodile suggests a dragon, but that animal lacks scales and many other features of the mythic counterpart – most importantly, the supple movement. Furthermore, crocodiles prey on mammals and birds, which the Chinese dragon never seems to do. Iguanids, geckos and chameleons, however, all share the ability to change colour with the Chinese dragon. Agamids, which are indigenous to China, often have crests or other ornaments, which can resemble the horns of Chinese dragons. Chameleons, as we have seen, even have considerable ability to change their shape, largely in order to redistribute their weight when climbing trees. Lizards swing their tails and shift every part of their bodies to maintain balance as they stride forwards, creating a sort of dance, which is taken up with great exuberance by the Chinese dragon. Were one to pick a single variety of lizard as the origin of the Asian dragon, it would be an agamid or chameleon, but the bringer of rain has been inspired by all of them. Images of the Chinese dragon spread though the Byzantine and Islamic worlds, and by the end of the fourteenth century, the Chinese dragon had become a common figure in Persian miniatures;[4] it soon began to influence Western art as well.

Though very ancient, the Western dragon does not seem to go back quite to the very beginnings of civilization. The European cave paintings of Spain and France concentrate on large mammals, and reptiles, especially smaller ones, are largely absent. Even crocodiles, whose size must have made them a constant danger for people, are very seldom or never depicted in cave art. Lizards are rare in ancient Egyptian art, though crocodiles, identified with Sobek and other deities, are very prominent.

But it is in Mesopotamia that the first clearly identifiable dragons emerge. Many depictions of deities and demons have at least some reptilian features, including those of Tiamat, a mother-goddess from whose body the world was created. Late in the third millennium BCE, a figure known as the 'mushussu' began to appear frequently. With scales, horns, claws, a tail, an extended neck and a forked tongue, it may be the first creature in the West to merit the name of 'dragon'. The general form and, most especially, the horns give it a resemblance to early Chinese dragons, suggesting

that the two may have a common origin, but the similarity could also easily be due to independent invention. Though certainly mythological, the mushussu resembles a monitor lizard more than any other existing creature.

But the Chinese dragon, despite occasionally causing floods and hurricanes, is generally benign, while the Western dragon is malignant. Many heroes and deities in the ancient world – including Nintura, Marduk, Apollo, Heracles, Cadmus, Perseus and Sigurd – are known for killing dragon-like figures. This iconography is repeated in the Christian world, where slayers of dragons

A variant of the mushussu from the Ishtar Gate, Istanbul, Turkey, dated to about 575 BCE.

include St George, St Margaret and Beowulf. In the Book of Revelation, both the Beast, which comes from the sea, and the False Prophet, who comes from the earth, are often identified as dragons.

It is in the late Middle Ages and Renaissance that Western dragons become particularly varied, colourful and interesting. The basic form of the dragon, which comes from a lizard, is adorned with all sorts of features taken from different creatures, such as the feathers of a peacock or the head of a dog. Dragons were also increasingly divided into categories such as the basilisk, the drake, the wyvern and so on. They began to lose some of their bad reputation as they became incorporated into the heraldic crests of noble families. In alchemy and some sorts of esoteric literature, dragons symbolized the spiritualization of matter. In the mid-sixteenth century, the clergyman Edward Topsell wrote, in a sort of taxonomy of dragons:

> There be some dragons which have wings and no feet, some again which have both feet and wings, and some neither feet nor wings, but are only distinguished from the common serpent by the comb growing on their heads and the beard under their cheeks . . . Besides, there are dragons of sundry colours, for some of them are black, some red, some of an ash colour, some yellow, and have their shape and outward appearance very beautiful . . . [5]

Dragons, in other words, shared not only the basic form but the diversity of lizards.

This was the Age of Exploration. The idea that all animals could fit into Noah's Ark had obscured the vast diversity of living things. But explorers were journeying across the globe and

Paolo Uccello, *St George and the Dragon*, 1456. This dragon has wings like those of a bat, adorned with a design from a peacock feather. The face is that of a dog, but with teeth like those of a snake. The general morphology, however, is definitely that of a lizard, and, moving on two legs, it anticipates later images of dinosaurs.

Winged dragon, from Topsell and Moffet's *History of Four-footed Beasts, Serpents and Insects* (1658).

bringing back vivid though confused accounts of exotic fauna, including brilliantly coloured chameleons, splendidly ornamented iguanas and enormous monitors. Early zoologists equated the new creatures with legendary beasts, from satyrs to mermaids. Despite systematic cataloguing of the newly discovered fauna and flora, the illustrations to travel books were often no less fantastic than paintings of ancient myths. In addition to the new creatures, Europeans were exposed to art from East Asia, the Islamic World and the New World. The motif of bats' wings on demons was introduced to the West from China during the late Middle Ages, and soon extended to dragons as well.[6]

But the 'salamander', a prominent lizard in the lore of the Renaissance, inherited a reputation going back at least to Aristotle, Pliny the Elder and Aelian, who all remarked on its ability to resist, and even to put out, fire with its touch. The sixteenth-century physician Paracelsus believed that the salamander was a being of pure fire, according to him, akin to a will-o'-the-wisp. Most critics identify this creature with one known as the 'fire salamander', whose scientific name is *Salamandra* – a small amphibian that is usually black with yellow spots. It is indigenous to most of Europe, and thrives especially in woody, mountainous areas. The fire salamander secretes a chemical through its skin that retards fire, often just enough to give the animal time to escape from a crevice in a burning log. But whichever animal the ancient authors may have been speaking of, that amphibian has virtually no resemblance to pictures of the salamander prior to at least the middle of the seventeenth century – for one thing, the salamander of Renaissance lore is depicted with scales and claws, indicating that it is a reptile (that is, a lizard) rather than an amphibian. It also differs from *Salamandra* in having a long neck and a crest along its back.

The Renaissance salamander became the emblem of King Francis I (*r.* 1515–47), sometimes known as 'the father of French culture' for his role in encouraging the arts. He had a fire-breathing salamander, turning its back and starting to look over its shoulder, depicted directly beneath the royal crown. Flames also appeared around the creature, and seemed to emanate from its joints as they moved.

The picture was often accompanied by the motto *Nutrisco et extinguo* ('I nourish and extinguish'). On the simplest level, this saying referred to reports that the salamander could both generate and put out flames. It also alluded to the status of the king as an absolute monarch, who created, and might contravene, the social order. This was no doubt part of the reason why images of the salamander became as ubiquitous in the French court as those of the dragon were at the Chinese. Scores of heraldic salamanders were displayed at Francis's palace at Fontainebleau – on walls, gates, medallions and just about any available surface. But the motto suggested far more esoteric meanings as well.

Several pictorial similarities indicate that the salamander of Francis I was at least partly inspired by the oriental dragon, whose image had by then found its way to Western Europe. Unlike the Western dragon, the salamander was clearly benign. It was

associated with the king, much as the Asian dragon was associated with the Chinese emperor. Both also had ears pointing upwards and a camelid sort of snout. The salamander was generally painted gold, approximately the same colour as the imperial dragon of the Chinese court. The ability of the salamander to both engender and quench flame suggests the way a Chinese dragon controls the weather, simultaneously creating lightning and rain. In the West, occidental dragons, starting with the one killed by Beowulf, had begun to breathe fire. But the salamander, like the Chinese dragon, also generates flame simply by the kinetic energy of its movement. The salamander is not generally depicted in quite as dynamic poses as the Chinese dragon, but it is also generally shown twisting its supple body in an upward curve. Both figures suggested the mystical union of opposites, and each was the focus of much arcane alchemy and philosophy.

Carved salamander from the palace of Francis I in Fontainebleau, early 16th century.

Illustration to *Historia animalium* by Conrad Gessner (1669 edn). Above is what Gessner considered an accurate depiction of a salamander, and below is a popular image that he considered false.

DE SALAMANDRA.

Konrad Gesner (1516–1565) of Switzerland is sometimes known as 'the founder of modern zoology', since he attempted to classify and discuss all known animals in his *Historia animalium*, first published in 1551–8. Unlike most of his predecessors, Gesner was seriously concerned with accuracy, and included an extensive bibliography, but it was very unusual when, in an edition of 1560, he juxtaposed two pictures of a creature he called a 'salamander', in order to expose one as false. The first was a reasonably accurate drawing of the amphibian we know today as the fire salamander. The other, which Gesner considered fraudulent, had claws, a string of stars down its back and a mammalian face. The image that Gesner rejected had probably first appeared as an illustration to an account by Bernhard von Breydenbach of the Holy Land, published in 1486, but had then been copied in many contemporary books.[7]

Illustration of a salamander from *Secretorum chymicum* (1687). The salamander, as depicted in the palaces of Francis I, continued to be important in alchemy and the occult, long after French royalty had lost interest in it.

The ultimate model for Breydenbach's monster may be the Chinese dragon, which, as already mentioned, had been widely depicted in the Islamic world. The stars on the creature's back suggest that it may have originally been part of an astrological chart. Gesner stated in a caption to his illustration that the false salamander had been an astrological sign, and the dragon is the major figure of the Chinese zodiac. Though Gesner does not specifically mention Francis I, he may have wished also to debunk the pretensions of the French court by demystifying its mascot. Francis I was a fervent Catholic who antagonized his Huguenot subjects, and Gesner was a Protestant. We do not know what creature Aristotle and Pliny actually had in mind in their writings on the salamander, nor what animal, if any, inspired the images at Fontainebleau, but the name 'salamander' became attached to the amphibian depicted by Gesner. After Francis I, the kings of France used the fleur-de-lis rather than the salamander as their symbol.

The 'Rainbow Serpent' in the mythology of Australian Aborigines is not a relatively discrete figure such as Horus in Egyptian mythology or Raven in the Amerindian mythology of the northwest coast of the United States, but, rather, an anthropological construct. It was first identified by A. R. Radcliffe-Brown in an article of 1926 entitled 'The Rainbow Serpent Myth of Australia'. He argued that the Rainbow Serpent was based on the identification of the rainbow with an enormous snake, moving from one watering hole to another, which ran through many of the highly diverse mythologies of Aboriginal tribes of Australia. It was associated with rock crystal, which can refract light in the manner of a prism.

Since, however, many of the indigenous beliefs had been lost, and others had not been studied, Radcliffe-Brown had to fill in many gaps with conjectures. He also observed that the rainbow was not always identified with a serpent, but could be a fish or other animal. He concluded by observing that the Rainbow Spirit resembled the Chinese dragon, since both resided in lakes or ponds and controlled the weather.[8] This is an example of one of the many fascinating analogies that constantly arise in anthropology, which might be due to a common origin in remote times, independent creation in different places, cultural contacts that went largely unrecorded, archetypes embedded in the human mind or perhaps some combination of these factors.

The concept of the Rainbow Serpent has been accepted by most anthropologists, as well as widely disseminated in popular culture, but it is not without its controversies. Some Aborigines believe it distorts their culture through the projection of Western ideas and values. Others, who have become Christian, take pride in identifying the Rainbow Serpent with the Western concept of God. But fascinating though they may be, these debates are beyond the scope of this book.

Australia has a variety of lizards unequalled anywhere else in the world except, perhaps, Madagascar. Many of them, with their brilliant pigmentation and ability to change colour, appear more suggestive of a rainbow than any snake, and it seems easily possible that they could have at least influenced the concept of a Rainbow Serpent. We should remember that the Aboriginal tales set in Dreamtime are profoundly different from the sort of histories we are used to in Western culture, where identities are clearly delineated and lines of narrative are fixed. In many tales, the animals engage in human activities, such as paddling canoes or throwing spears. A snake may marry a lizard, and all manner of animals may give birth to human beings. The stories can blur lines of species, just as they do the divisions between the present, past and future.

One remarkable feature of the Chinese dragon is that it combines the opposing forces of fire and water harmoniously within

Pictures used by A. R. Radcliffe-Brown to illustrate his theory of the Rainbow Spirit in Australian Aboriginal myth, from the *Journal of the Royal Anthropological Association* (1926). Radcliffe-Brown assumed the animals depicted were snakes. In the top picture, at least, they could also have been monitor lizards viewed from above, since they are a bit wider around the middle and taper around their heads and tails.

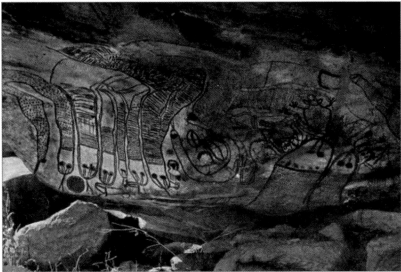

The Toltec
Temple of the
Feathered Serpent
in Xochicalco,
Mexico,
c. 650–900 CE.
The crest suggests
an iguana, but the
tongue is closer
to that of a tegu.

its person, to generate thunder, lightning and rain. In many tales
of the Australian Aborigines, by contrast, the Rainbow Serpent
represents water, while a lizard represents fire, making them
adversaries, though, in a sense, also partners in the creation of the
world. From Nelgi, an island off the coast of Australia near Cape
York, comes a story of how a frilled lizard named Walek brought
fire to his home. When smoke was seen over distant lands, the
lizards suspected that a special power had been discovered. Walek
swam to the place where the smoke began to ascend, took a coal
in its mouth and then returned, but the tongue of the frilled lizard
still bears a scar where it was burned.[9] Aborigines of the Bund-
jalung Nation in New South Wales trace their ancestry to Gonna,
a monitor lizard, that once quarrelled with the Rainbow Serpent.
As the lizard pursued the snake, the pair created rivers and mountains out of the formless earth.[10] This tale probably refers to a
storm that brought torrential rain and flooding, creating channels
for water and mounds of earth.

The lizard, as we have already seen, resembles a huge range of creatures, from fish to insects and anteaters, and, at times, almost seems to contain all other animals. A snake is a lizard without legs; a mammal is a lizard with fur; a bird is a lizard with wings; a dragon is a huge lizard, and so, for that matter, is a dinosaur. In traditional tales, it can be difficult to tell a lizard from a crocodile, a snake or even a human being, and so the lizard becomes a sort of default form for composite creatures.

The feathered serpent is a figure found in many Mesoamerican cultures, and its ubiquity and importance parallels that of the Asian and Western dragons, the Rainbow Serpent of Australia and the Chameleon of southern Africa (described below). The Aztecs called it 'Quetzalcoatl', the Yucatec Maya 'Kukulkan'. In *Popol Vuh*, the religious epic of the Quiché Maya, it is the deity 'Qucumatz' who creates the world and humankind.[11] Representations of the feathered serpent, mostly carved in stone, often show appendages such as arms, as well as adornments such as a crest or frill around the neck. Many of the figures are very stylized, and it is not always easy to distinguish the various body parts or even to tell scales from plumes. But, like the dragons of other regions, the feathered serpent is often associated with water and with storms, and goes back almost to the beginning of the cosmos. The people who first crossed the Bering Strait from Asia and populated the Americas could have brought a mythology with some variant of the Chinese dragon.

A fastidious neatness in Western culture moves us to place even fantastic creatures in elaborate classificatory schemes. In the Book of Leviticus, animals are classed as 'clean' and 'unclean' on the basis of such apparently arbitrary features as whether they ruminate or have split hooves. Taxonomy becomes more elaborate in Aristotle, and then almost obsessively complex in the work of Linnaeus and his successors. Mythological figures of Western culture such as the centaur or sphinx can generally be relatively easily broken down into their component species. The Amerindian imagination, particularly in South and Central America, is more phantasmagoric. Identities and species seem to appear, merge and separate, a bit like sounds and images in the rainforest.

European cosmology divides consciousness into units, which correspond to the bodies of different human beings and other living things. For Mesoamericans, by contrast, sentience is an underlying unity, while the body is a temporary, and relatively superficial, division. A single body may be occupied by several souls, while a soul may have several bodies. This also means that no living thing – whether human, animal or deity – is defined by its physical appearance.[12] It is hard to separate the various species that may have contributed to the image of the feathered serpent. It is legitimate to call it, at least in many representations, a 'fantastic lizard', though it is not easy to be sure how much the images may owe to, say, an iguana or a gila monster.

The green iguana is a huge creature that spends most of its time in trees and, with its dramatic crest and bright colour, certainly seems imposing enough to be taken for a plumed serpent. A legend of the Cora Indians in west-central Mexico tells that the iguana, in a fit of anger, once took all the fire in the world and hoarded it in the sky. The people were cold, and at first asked birds to retrieve the fire. Both the raven and the hummingbird tried, but neither could fly high enough. Then the opossum agreed, and told people that it would knock the fire down from heaven, but that the people must wait and catch the flame with blankets before it could reach the earth. The opossum climbed through trees until it reached the sky, and the iguana took the form of an old man, who allowed the visitor to rest by the fire. The opossum knocked flames down to earth with its tail, and people failed to catch them, so the earth was burned, but, ever since, humankind has kept possession of fire.[13]

There are dragons in the lore of the North American Amerindians as well. One, known as the 'Piasa', was seen by explorer Jacques Marquette in 1673, painted on a limestone bluff overlooking the Mississippi River in Illinois. He described it as a fantastic, though very lizard-like, creature, having scales, a human face, a deer's horns and a long tail that wound around its body. Father Marquette was initially frightened by the sight, and then later marvelled at the skill of the painters, saying that the undertaking would challenge any artists in his native France. The figure has since been destroyed and repainted. Similar figures in Native American art around the Mississippi River suggest that, like many dragons of the Old World, it may have been the spirit of a pond or lake.[14]

This iguana looks very much at home among the remains of Mayan pyramids, Yucatán Peninsula, Mexico.

The chameleon seems like no other animal, with its huge eyes that focus separately, its changes of colour, its adjustments of shape and the enormous speed and precision with which it can

catch insects with its tongue. Part of the fascination with the chameleon is that it mirrors human alienation from the natural world, which has long been a source of both loneliness and vanity. Pride in our apparent uniqueness as a species is an essential part of all claims to human exceptionalism. At the same time, we are constantly troubled by our resulting sense of alienation from animals and nature. In many African mythologies, the chameleon, in a similar way, is solitary, powerful and isolated from other creatures. Perhaps the chameleon is a lizard in about the way, or to the same degree, that a human being is an ape.

In myths of the Bantu peoples of sub-Saharan Africa, the chameleon is often the oldest of animals. According to accounts of the

Native American petroglyph showing a lizard by an artist of the Fremont culture, Dinosaur National Park, Utah, c. 1000 BCE. It is impossible to know whether the impression is intentional or not, but the lizard appears to be swimming in a pond.

Drawing based on the reconstructed rock painting of the 'Piasa'. The original image, according to some accounts, did not have wings.

Senufo people of the Ivory Coast, the chameleon walks so slowly because, when it first appeared in the world, the soil was permeated with primeval waters and very soft. According to legends of the Yoruba of Nigeria, God assigned the chameleon, the orisha (patron deity) of medicine, to test the solidity of the earth before the arrival of human beings, and that is why it takes every step so deliberately.[15]

According to a tale of the Malawi people of eastern Central Africa, the chameleon was once the only creature on earth. It felt lonely and climbed very high in a tree, searching for a companion. After a meal of fruit, the chameleon fell asleep, and an intense wind knocked it to the ground. When the chameleon landed and burst apart, all other living things, including human beings, came out of its body.

The Bantu peoples generally believe in a supreme God, who is similar to that of the Abrahamic religions, but has withdrawn from the world. There are many myths about this departure, which is often due to transgressions or mistakes of humankind, for example by starting fires or by making noise. The chameleon often serves as a mediator between the distant God and human beings, as well as between people and animals.[16]

A very widespread tale in several Bantu cultures makes the chameleon a messenger of eternal life, whose good news, however, is contradicted by an adversary, which may be an agama lizard, hare or other animal. According to a version from the Wute people of Cameroon, God entrusted the chameleon with a message that people would die yet afterwards rise from their graves. As was his habit, the chameleon climbed down from heaven to earth very slowly through the branches of a tree, often pausing to reflect. A snake had overheard the message and decided to play a trick on men and women. It quickly slithered down the trunk of the tree, and then told people that their deaths would be forever.

Death himself was listening, took the words as an invitation, and immediately began to take the spirits of men and women. When the chameleon finally arrived, people were confused and refused to believe its message. Eventually, the chameleon and the snake took their case before God, who cursed the snake for having lied. But it was too late to take back the power of Death. To this day, people kill snakes in revenge for being deprived of immortality.[17] Each of the countless versions of this story gives another twist to an ongoing dialectic of life and mortality, creation and annihilation.

Many regard the chameleon with ambivalence. The Malawi honour the animal but fear its power, and there is a widespread belief that the bite of a chameleon can turn a man into a snake.[18] The chameleon usually stands for the vital principle, though that is reversed among the Bangwa people of western Cameroon. They

Marten de Vos and Adriaen Collaert, *Africa*, 1586–91. Here, Africa is represented by a woman riding proudly on a fanciful crocodile, framed by a chameleon on the left and either snakes or legless lizards on the right.

tell of how the chameleon, in a fit of anger, once declared that all living things must perish, but a toad softened this by saying that they would be reborn. Accordingly, we go through a continual cycle of birth and passing away. The chameleon, representing fire, is paired with the frog or toad, representing water, and together they bring rain.[19] But, for Bantu Christians, the chameleon can even be an avatar of Christ.

For Europeans of the early modern period, Africa, even more than the Americas, was the magical continent. It was the place where one might encounter griffins, men with the necks and heads of cranes or even the gods of ancient Egypt. Taken from Africa to the western world as an exotic pet, the chameleon retained its reputation as a sorcerer. The ability of the chameleon to change colour is truly amazing, but, until at least the middle of the twentieth century, it was both misunderstood and exaggerated. The chameleon changes colour for many reasons, but the males actually do this far more often to stand out, in order to impress the females, than to blend in with their environment. In popular culture, however, chameleons obtained a reputation for camouflaging themselves so well as to become invisible. In the words of Carolyn Wells, 'If there is nothing on the tree/ 'Tis the Chameleon you see.'[20]

But perhaps Wells, even if she did not consciously realize this, was speaking of mythic dragons. Most people do not quite believe in fairies, ghosts or nature spirits, yet they do not entirely disbelieve in them either. Such figures hover, a bit like the physicist

Flap-neck chameleon moving slowly and deliberately among the leaves of an acacia tree, South Africa.

Jan van Vianen, *Cupid Holding a Chameleon*, 1686. The way a chameleon changes colour and form is associated with alchemy, shape-shifters and the transformative power of love. It is a bit hard to say, however, whether the message of this print is romantic or cynical.

24 Emblemes d'Amour

Jan Luyken, *Two Men see a Chameleon*, 1711. The sight of a chameleon, and of many other lizards, is still enough to make people stop and gaze in amazement.

J. J. Grandville, illustration to *Scènes de la vie privée et publique des animaux* (1842). This chameleon in parliament constantly changes his views, as those in the forest change their colours, so as to always be with the majority.

Schrödinger's cat (whose life depended on the indeterminate position of an electron), between existence and non-existence, in what we sometimes call 'the realm of the imagination'.

What is the difference between the lizard and the dragon? We might call the gap 'myth' or 'metaphor', and it is not always easy to distinguish between the two. Philosophers have shown that the simple act of naming an animal involves many covert assumptions, which come very close to mythologizing. Lizards not only have the physical features that human beings usually associate with dragons such as scales, long tails and sinuous torsos, but play the role of dragons in a sort of miniature world. They pursue or ambush insects with the ferocity of dragons. For many of them, apart from the matter of scale, a clump of weeds and grass is like the primeval forest, where one might expect dragons to be found.

4 Lizards and Dinosaurs

Future Angels to whom the Wars and Destructions of Time
are unknown, shall seek throughout the limitless Empires of
Space their ghastly remains, and finding amongst them the
self-same Weapons of which we speak, be curious in remote
centenaries to hear anew the Tale of the Dragons.
Thomas Hawkins, *Book of Great Sea Dragons, Ichthyosauri and
Plesiosauri* (1840)

From very early times, the idea of an 'Age of Reptiles' has run
through Western culture. In the Babylonian creation epic, the
goddess–demon Tiamat gives birth to a series of largely reptilian
monsters, who defend her rule until she is finally killed by the
supreme god Marduk. In Greek mythology, Tiamat becomes
Gaia or 'Mother Earth'. She gives birth to the Titans, described
by Hesiod as fantastic, reptilian creatures. They make war upon,
and are eventually defeated by, Zeus and the other anthropomorphic deities. A Parthian scripture of Zoroastrianism, the first
of the great dualistic faiths, recounts that reptiles were created
not by Ahura Mazda, the principle of good, but by his adversary
Ahriman, the embodiment of evil:

And upon the earth he let loose reptiles in corporeal form
– and they mingled with each other – reptiles, biting and
poisonous – the serpent-dragon, scorpion, venomous lizard,
tortoise, and frog, so that not so much as a needle's point on
the whole earth remained free from reptiles.[1]

The Bible contains two accounts of Creation. In the first,
human beings are created after the animals, but are then placed
in charge of them. In the second, the animals are created after
Adam but before Eve, in the hope that they might be suitable

Androgynous
image of Tiamat
from an Assyrian
relief from the
library of King
Ashurbanipal,
c. 668–626 BCE.

companions for the first man. In the second account, the Serpent
of Eden, the only creature to speak in the Bible (if you do not
count Balaam's ass), seems to have a status beyond that of the
other animals, suggesting that it may once have had, or at least
aspired to, a human sort of dominion.

As we start to approach the modern period, this age when
reptiles reigned supreme – under the rule of Tiamat, Gaia, Ahura
Mazda or the Serpent of Eden – continues in the collective

imagination as the period before the Great Flood and Noah's Ark. It is remembered as a time of wickedness, since God found it necessary to punish man and the world, but also – simply because it took place in biblical times – as holy. The association of giant lizards – that is, dragons – with apocalyptic terrors, which goes back to very early times, is perhaps most memorably expressed in the biblical Book of Revelation, where the dragon sweeps a third of the stars from the sky with its tail.

Long before the discovery of dinosaurs, dragons in Western iconography have been associated with the past, and those who slew them were symbols of modernity. When St George killed the dragon, it represented a triumph of Christianity, the new religion, over an anachronistic paganism. St Margaret of Antioch was the daughter of a pagan priest. When she converted to Christianity, her father was enraged. She refused to renounce her faith, so he fed his daughter to a dragon. When Margaret made the sign of the cross in its belly, the dragon burst open, and she re-emerged. She was 'born again', like the new religion emerging from the ruin of the old. The motif of a world dominated by lizards and other reptiles constantly resurfaces in new contexts, among them the representation of prehistoric life.

As the Industrial Revolution progressed, the expansion of mining and quarrying uncovered fossils on an unprecedented scale. When dinosaurs were gradually discovered around the end of the eighteenth century, they were disconcerting not only because of their enormous size and unfamiliar forms, but because they did not fit easily into the tidy world of Linnaean classifications. They inspired a very vibrant series of debates, which blended biology, theology, earth science, myth and many other areas of study. The motif of an Age of Reptiles, long established in Western culture, provided the foundation for our images of dinosaurs.

St Margaret of Antioch slaying a dragon, illustration from *Wittenberger Heiligtumbuch* (1509). The young lady rises serenely out of the dragon's side, and the new religion is triumphant.

The scientific disputes about dinosaurs in the eighteenth and early nineteenth centuries were conducted on a high intellectual level, yet researchers were trying to reconstruct primeval monsters, together with their entire world, on the basis of the very little evidence available. Lizards offered a very rich heritage of images that people could draw on. In many ways, the model was misleading, and, up until the later twentieth century, people mistakenly portrayed most dinosaurs as walking on all fours and dragging their tails on the ground in the manner of lizards.

In 1841 the term Dinosauria for the newly discovered class of enormous reptiles was coined by the palaeontologist Richard Owen (1804–1892), from the Greek *deinos*, meaning 'terrible', and *sauros*, meaning 'lizard'. Owen added that the dinosaurs might have had four-chambered hearts like mammals and been warm blooded and far more active than the lizards we know today.[2] But, if the differences were so considerable, why did he call them 'lizards' at all? For one thing, creatures alive in the modern era offered the only framework for classification that was available, and lizards were easily the most well-developed template. In addition, Owen was a determined adversary of the emerging idea of evolution, which advocates in that era generally assumed was a matter of progressive improvement. He wished to suggest that, since the lizards of the remote past were vastly larger and more

Bones of a plesiosaur buried in a hill as depicted in a French book on natural history, early to mid-19th century.

impressive than those today, an evolutionary link between them and creatures like the iguana was impossible. But dragons of legend were also warm-blooded, so much so that they could often breathe fire, so Owen was, in a sense, unconsciously following a mythic tradition. Essentially, people had imagined dinosaurs, just as they had the dragons, as lizards plus something else. These lizards might, in other words, possess the wings of bats, faces of dogs or limbs of human beings, while remaining reptilian in essence.

Today, 'dinosaur', much like 'fish' or 'lizard', is no longer a recognized scientific category. It is still very common in popular culture, as a sort of umbrella term for many creatures that lived in a certain era and were not necessarily very closely related. Most are now divided into Saurischia – meaning 'lizard hips' – including Tyrannosaurus rex and Apatosaurus (a.k.a., 'brontosaurus'), and Ornithischia, or 'bird hips', including Triceratops and Stegosaurus. Scientific language, as we have already seen, has ever-fewer points of contact with popular culture. Were dinosaurs lizards? The question is not entirely meaningful in the context of contemporary science. If we understand the terms 'dinosaur' and 'lizard' in more restrictive ways, we will probably answer in the negative. Lepidosauria, the evolutionary lineage that would lead to squamates (including monitors, geckos, lacertids, iguanas and so on) and tuataras, diverged from Archosaura, the lineage that would lead to dinosaurs, in the early Permian era, which began 299 million years ago. Archosaura then split into Dinosauria, the lineage of dinosaurs, and Crocodilia (including crocodiles, alligators and gharials) around the beginning of the Triassic period, 251 million years ago. The only animals known to palaeontologists of the early nineteenth century that were evolutionary ancestors of the animals that scientists now generally call 'lizards' were aquatic giants such as mosasaurs and plesiosaurs. Nevertheless, traditional usage, naive perception and poetic associations concur in identifying dinosaurs with lizards. When we look at an iguana, we see a miniature dinosaur.

The Victorian era was a period of rapid industrialization and scientific innovation, but the prevailing ideology in England was one of nostalgic romanticism. The huge lizard-like figures invoked the demons of medieval lore, evoking a dimly remembered Age of Faith. They also brought to mind combats of knights and dragons, and, in consequence, the Age of Chivalry. The idea of geologic time, in which the dinosaurs had lived, seemed romantic in its vastness, even if it was disorientating. Perhaps most of all, the dinosaurs had a romantic appeal through their association with severe, forbidding landscapes, which the Victorians considered sublime. In the words of Donald Worster,

> On every hand, in painting, poetry, and music, a super-abundance of terror was presented: roaring lions leaping onto the backs of paralyzed stallions, dreadful torrents plunging over cliffs, thundering volcanoes erupting into lurid skies.[3]

Like artists, scientists borrowed traditional imagery of catastrophic horror from representations of hell or of remote places where nature, in all its magnificent savagery, still reigned supreme. Georges Cuvier (1769–1832), the leading palaeontologist of the early nineteenth century, believed that Noah's Flood was only the last in a series of catastrophes in which life was destroyed and then recreated. This series of extinctions accounted for the existence of varied creatures in different strata of rock. To quote Worster once more,

> As depicted by the French paleontologist Georges Cuvier, these convulsions (of the earth) took on a terrific, awesome

splendor. Mountains exploded, seas boiled, and monstrous creatures were buried in rumbling avalanches.[4]

Palaeontologists of the early nineteenth century, especially the British and French, projected the violence of their own era, including the Napoleonic Wars and the imperial wars of conquest, into remote times. The catastrophism of Cuvier, especially, was influenced by the turbulent succession of governments in France, where the king and queen had been decapitated, as were many of their revolutionary successors, including Danton and Robespierre. Cuvier and his contemporaries used the word 'revolution' (the same in French and English) to refer to both geological and political upheavals. Scientists and popularizers viewed the reign of dinosaurs in terms of essentially the same struggle between the old order and the new, which they saw in European countries and their colonies. The great lizards of the past were the *ancien régime*, imposing in their grandeur yet always fighting one another, and doomed to give way to successors who were more proficient in the use of reason.

Nevertheless, the theory of catastrophism did not render emphasis on violence inevitable. Instead of devastation, scientists could have emphasized the relatively stable periods between mass extinctions. Instead of violent deaths, they could have pointed out that the vast size of dinosaurs suggested they had long lives. Many scientists of the late eighteenth and nineteenth centuries probably unconsciously sabotaged the easy acceptance of their theories by indulging a bit too freely in a taste for romantic horror, thus scaring away much of the public.

Those leviathans were imagined mostly as giant lizards, and their world was one of unrestrained predation. This idea was popularized in a barely coherent work by Thomas Hawkins entitled *The Book of Great Sea Dragons, Ichthyosauri and Plesiosauri*, published in 1840, in which the author compared the newly discovered dinosaurs to monsters of biblical lore. He called the dragons 'sharp-fanged and murdering creatures of the deep abundant'.[5] Towards the end of the book, Hawkins added,

> The huge carnivorous Races found in Caverns and gravel-beds have a second moral from whence it is impossible to escape, and the Earth is filled with uncounted Ruin, but ill-concealed with flowers.[6]

With hardly a pause, Hawkins assailed the reader with non-stop images of blood, infernos, landslides, tempests and earthquakes. He saw the destruction of the dragons as an expression of the wrath of God, and, in consequence, an admonition to humankind.

The frontispiece of the book was by John Martin (1798–1854), a painter previously known for imposing tableaux of biblical disasters. It is entitled 'Sea Dragons and How They Lived', and shows dinosaurs on a desolate shore in an orgy of predatory violence. On the right, one pterodactyl plucks an eye from a freshly killed ichthyosaurus, while others bite into the victim's sides. On the left, one plesiosaurus faces off against two ichthyo-sauri, all three of which are baring their enormous teeth. Around them, the dark waves churn and lash in the moonlight. This image, together with others by Martin, would become the model for illustrations of dinosaurs for many decades to come.

Writing in 1850, the poet Alfred, Lord Tennyson (1809–1892), in 'In Memoriam', expressed the existential insecurity brought on by the new scientific discoveries, which would soon reach an apex in the reaction to the publication of Darwin's *Origin of Species* nine years later. If, as geologists such as Charles Lyell had shown, even mountains were subject to change, they could no longer be sym-bols of eternity. And if, as catastrophists such as Georges Cuvier had argued, species were subject to eventual extinction, we could no longer rely with any confidence on the indefinite survival of humankind.

In section LVI, Tennyson makes one of the earliest poetic references to dinosaurs, though he refers to them as 'dragons'. In typical Victorian fashion, he contrasts their savage existence with human idealism:

John Martin, frontispiece to *The Book of Great Sea Dragons, Ichthyosauri and Plesiosauri* by Thomas Hawkins (1840). Early writers on fossils mostly viewed the era of dinosaurs as one of total chaos and uninterrupted violence.

Who trusted God was love indeed
And love Creation's final law –
Tho' Nature red in tooth and claw
With ravine, shriek'd against this creed –

Who loved, who suffered countless ills,
Who battled for the True, the Just,

Be blown about the desert dust,
Or seal'd within the iron hills?

No more? A monster then, a dream,
A discord. Dragons of the prime,
That tare [sic] each other in their slime,
Where mellow music match'd with him.[7]

Tennyson contemplated the dinosaurs as a sort of mirror image of humanity, with a blend of horror and sympathy. Men and women professed high ideals, but was that enough to distinguish us? Like the dinosaurs, we could be extremely violent, and perhaps we as well were headed towards extinction in the end.

People had been coming across fossilized bones of dinosaurs and great mammals from time immemorial, and these bones contributed to legends of dragons, giants and other creatures. Since they were always fragmentary, they could not easily tell people much more than that the creatures in question were often of enormous size. Fossils were collected in the curio cabinets of rulers and aristocrats during the Age of Exploration. In the modern period, the recording and study of these fossils gradually became more systematic.

Until around the end of the seventeenth century, people had generally assumed, despite occasional dissent, that species corresponded to unchanging archetypes and were, therefore, immutable. When bones of the mastodon were dug up in Kentucky, Ohio and South Carolina, the creature was called the 'American elephant', and researchers expected that it would soon be discovered in the flesh. This was part of the mission of Lewis and Clark, who were delegated by Jefferson to explore the Northwest Territories in 1804.

Perhaps the first primeval lizard to be examined scientifically was discovered in about 1775, when a soldier came across a huge fossilized skull in a chalk quarry near the city of Maastricht in the Netherlands. It was revered as a relic of the period before the biblical Great Flood, but variously identified as belonging to several creatures, from a giant crocodile to a whale. The skull was confiscated by invading French soldiers in 1795, taken back to Paris and presented to Cuvier. Primarily on the basis of its teeth, he ascertained that the creature was an aquatic lizard. It was eventually named 'Mosasaurus', meaning 'lizard of the Maas river', and is now considered an ancestor of monitors, geckos and other lizards.

The most celebrated fossil of the first half of the nineteenth century was a herbivorous creature of previously unimaginably vast proportions, first discovered on a rural road in Sussex by Mary Ann Mantell (1795–1855) in 1822, and then later analysed by her husband Gideon Mantell (1790–1852). On the basis of the teeth, Gideon determined that it resembled an iguana, named it 'iguanodon' or 'iguana-tooth', and estimated its length at 21 m (70 ft). In reconstructing the skeleton, he mistakenly placed a claw

John Martin, *The Evening of the Deluge*, 1828. For Martin, biblical times, with their floods and plagues, were not so different from primordial worlds. The fallen angels and demons were even a bit like dinosaurs.

on the nose, giving it a horn a bit like that of a rhinoceros. Even this error, however, was inspired by comparison of the skeleton with iguanas, which, he pointed out, often 'have horny protuberances on the head and snout'.[8] In a sketch, Mantell depicted the creature as a giant iguana, complete with a very long tail and appendages that, rather than being directly beneath its body, splayed outwards to the sides.[9]

The iguanodon would become the centrepiece of the islands of dinosaurs in the Crystal Palace Exhibition in London that opened in 1851. This was part of an enormous fair, in which all countries were invited to display their accomplishments in science, industry and culture. The vast production featured science, showmanship, industry, fantasy and commerce, united by an ideology of human progress and an ambience a bit like that of Disneyland

John Martin, *The Country of the Iguanodon*, 1837. This watercolour is the frontispiece for Gideon Mantell's *The Principles of Geology*. A sole iguanodon is engaged in an unequal struggle against two megalosauri, in a world of constant and unrestrained predation.

today. The artificial islands featured extinct animals of various ages, as they had been identified by fossils in different strata of rock. Except for the island of great mammals, all were essentially conceived as lizards. The official *Guide to the Crystal Palace and Park* of 1856 referred to the ichthyosaurus as a 'fish lizard' and the plesiosaurus as a 'serpent lizard'.[10]

The models were built by Benjamin Waterhouse Hawkins (1807–1894). He constructed each around an iron frame, using immense quantities of cement, tile and stone. The centrepiece of the entire project was the iguanodon, which measured almost 11 m (35 ft) in length.[11] Gideon Mantell had conceived the animal as, apart from the horn on its nose, nearly identical to an iguana, but it would have been difficult to make a model of the relatively slender body of an iguana, including the long tail, that would have been sufficiently sturdy. Instead, Hawkins, guided by Richard Owen, made the legs thicker and more clearly muscular, placed them directly underneath the torso, and gave the model a comparatively short but heavy tail.

To a certain extent, the islands of extinct creatures were designed to appeal to visitors as a sort of 'house of horrors'. The sculptures of even herbivorous animals such as the iguanodon emphasized their large teeth – so much so that the public at times took them for carnivores.[12] The highly muscled bodies, huge claws, menacing poses and intense eyes all contributed to a fearsome impression. A cartoon in *Punch* of 1855 showed a pompous schoolmaster leading an utterly terrified little boy by the hand among the giant lizards, as a sardonic comment on the educational value of the models.[13] Nevertheless, Hawkins always endeavoured not to go too far in frightening or upsetting the public, and the Crystal Palace Park was like a child-friendly adventure film. His dinosaurs often had vaguely threatening postures, but were never actually shown engaged in predation. By constantly suggesting violence but never

Print showing Benjamin Waterhouse Hawkins working on his sculptures of the iguanodon and other dinosaurs in his Sydenham studio, c. 1854. The bird on a plank supporting the palaeotherium on the left and the rats on the floor provide a contrast with the giants of old.

actually showing it, Hawkins may have given the impression that dinosaurs were clumsy and sluggish.

The theme park devoted to extinct animals officially opened in 1854 to great public acclaim. Although the models were rendered obsolete within a few years by new palaeontological discoveries,

Cartoon by John Leech showing a teacher dragging a terrified boy through an exhibit of the Crystal Palace dinosaurs, from the *Punch Almanack* (1855). The dinosaurs were intended, like the 'house of horrors' at an amusement park, to scare people a little but not too much.

they never lost their popularity and are still visited today. They inspired the fascination with dinosaurs that is still with us, as well as popular images of them as enormous lizards that, though altered in many details over the decades, still set the tone in popular culture.

The climax of the opening was a dinner on the last day of 1853 for 21 guests, mostly scientists and officials, inside a model of the iguanodon. There was a good deal of drinking, and the visitors sang many songs, including one with the following verse:

A thousand ages underground,
His skeleton had lain,
But now his body's big and round
And there's life in him again.

Chorus:
The jolly old beast
Is not deceased.
There's life in him again! (roar).[14]

The message here was, at least in part, a denial of the finality of extinction, a prospect that had been so distressing to Tennyson and others.

The Crystal Palace Park strongly suggested the idea of actually revisiting the Age of Reptiles, which might, perhaps, have survived in some remote part of the world. The first of many fictional accounts of this may have been the novel *Journey to the Centre of the Earth* by Jules Verne (1828–1905), first published in 1864, a decade after the opening of the Crystal Palace Park. It was inspired partly by the idea that strata in rocks contained the remnants of early geological epochs, which suggested that, by descending deep into the earth, it might be possible to rediscover those eras.

The book described a battle of primeval titans, a theme that had already been depicted by artists such as John Martin and was strongly suggested, if never quite shown, by the sculptures at the Crystal Palace Park. The narrator, after descending into a volcano with other explorers, witnesses a combat between an ichthyosaurus and a plesiosaurus:

John Weeks, *Nature's Gathering*, 1854. The picture shows an iguana on a rock above a sailfin dragon – both lizards were major models for the Crystal Park dinosaurs. They have very different ranges, and neither is indigenous to Europe, so the European castle in the background seems incongruous.

Benjamin Waterhouse Hawkins, *Dinner in the Mould of the Iguanodon*, 1853–4. Viewed symbolically, the picture is a bit hard to interpret. Who is devouring whom?

Two monsters only made all this commotion in the sea, and I really beheld two reptiles of the primitive age . . . These animals fought with incredible fury; they raised mountainous waves . . .

The combat lasts for several hours of unabated rage, and then the plesiosaurus raises its vast head above the water, showing a mortal wound, to fall back in death with a huge splash.[15]

For the Victorians, such fury in combat appeared primitive and, therefore, appropriate to reptiles of the deep. In fact, fights among reptiles are usually over rather quickly, and, when there is no immediate victor, they do not have the desire to prolong them. Verne's lizards of the deep seem almost human, in that they engage in battle for no very apparent reason and continue to the death.

The image of the two monsters reflects Darwinian ideas about competition among species, as well as popular notions of 'dominance'. The ichthyosaurus and plesiosaurus are battling, in a way that is very anthropomorphic, to be ruler of the sea. But when we say that human beings are now the 'dominant species', what

114

exactly do we mean? Perhaps we mean that human beings are becoming more numerous, but we are far less so than ants or snails. Jellyfish go back almost to the beginning of life on this planet, and their numbers, already far ahead of ours, are increasing. Or perhaps it means that humans have the power to alter their environment, but some of that freedom may be an illusion, since we find it very hard to change even our own institutions. And when we say that dinosaurs were 'dominant' during the Jurassic period, we are generally using completely different criteria – physical size and biological diversity.

In 2008, there was even a weekly show on the American History Channel called *Jurassic Fight Club*, which featured bloody combats among dinosaurs generated by computer, such as 'allosaurus versus ceratosaurus' or 'giganotosaurus versus tyrannosaurus'. A narrator would call the moves, much as at a mixed martial arts match, commenting on strategy and tactics. When one dinosaur was victorious, the announcer would often tell the audience that the victory was only short-term, since the winner would soon fall victim to other attackers, disease or starvation.

Dinosaurs from *Johnson's Natural History* (1867). Some are copied from pictures by John Martin, but they are arranged in novel ways. As had become the convention, their bodies are heaped up and entangled, as they constantly endeavour to bite one another.

For the Victorians, the world of the dinosaurs had been one of primeval chaos. The enormous lizards embodied the destructive force of nature, as revealed in violent tempests, earthquakes and volcanic eruptions. By the middle of the twentieth century, human beings were starting to gain powers on almost a comparable scale, especially with the creation of nuclear weapons. During the Cold War, people on both sides of the conflict lived with the perpetual fear of a nuclear war, perhaps capable of annihilating all of humankind, which might break out at any moment.

In 1954, Toho Studios in Japan released its film *Godzilla*, which, consciously or not, continued the Victorian traditions of romantic terror. In the movie, Godzilla is a giant lizard, which has been roused from the depths of the sea by underwater testing of hydrogen bombs. It rampages through Tokyo, knocking down large buildings. Finally, after several failed attempts, the Japanese army kills Godzilla with a biological weapon, but a scientist warns that further nuclear testing might awaken other monsters.

Illustration to Jules Verne's *Journey to the Centre of the Earth* showing a plesiosaurus fighting an ichthyosaurus (1864).

Poster for the film *Godzilla* in the original Japanese, released in 1954. At the time, the memory of the bombing of Hiroshima, Nagasaki and many other Japanese cities was still fresh in people's memories, so the bombers and the flaming buildings could evoke raw emotions.

Godzilla is modelled mostly after Tyrannosaurus rex, but with a row of spines like those of a stegosaurus down its back. Like Japanese dragons, it has four claws and lives deep in the sea. Like Western dragons, it breathes fire, though in the form of a ray. For all its destructiveness, the monster is, like the people of Hiroshima and Nagasaki, a victim of nuclear weapons. Played by an actor in a lizard costume, the creature projected pathos through its gestures, and audiences were sad to see it die.

The movie was a huge commercial success, and launched a series of spin-offs, which is probably far from over. Godzilla has been matched against many other giants, including King Kong. In the movie *Godzilla versus Hedora* of 1971, Godzilla became the defender of humanity against the 'Smog Monster', an antagonist created from industrial pollution. Though often victorious, the giant lizard has also been repeatedly killed and resurrected. Perhaps most importantly, the original Godzilla film established a cinematic tradition in which the primordial giants that once ruled the earth return to avenge human crimes against nature.

For all of the scientific discoveries in the last century and a half, the popular view of dinosaurs as enhanced lizards seems to have changed remarkably little. The palaeontologist Robert Bakker helped to inspire another in a long series of public waves of enthusiasm for extinct leviathans by publishing a sort of manifesto in the issue of *Discovery* from spring 1968 entitled 'The Superiority of Dinosaurs'. The first mammals, little rodent-like creatures, appeared around the beginning of the Triassic period (205 million years ago), about 20 million years before the first dinosaurs. Since people understood evolution as progressive improvement through natural selection, this seemed to pose a problem. If dinosaurs were essentially lizards like those we know today, how was it possible that they were able to outcompete mammals and become the dominant creatures on the planet? How were they able to become so large, diverse and numerous?[16]

Bakker's answer is that dinosaurs actually resembled the mammals of today. They were endothermic (that is, warm-blooded), and thereby able to maintain a high level of energy, in addition to being more intelligent than many scientists had previously believed.[17] After extensive debates, a consensus emerged among palaeontologists that the bones simply did not provide enough evidence to tell with any confidence how dinosaurs regulated their body temperature. There was, however, a new appreciation of the complexity of the question.

The entire dichotomy of ectothermic (that is, cold-blooded) and endothermic began to appear overly simplistic. Animals regulate their body temperature in many ways, and may even do so in different ways at different stages in their lives. Bees raise their temperature by shivering their muscles. Chameleons, iguanas and other lizards darken their colour to retain heat better. Fish and other ectotherms release chemicals to prevent them from freezing in cold weather. Both reptiles and mammals lower their body temperature during hibernation. Human beings may be endotherms, yet we regulate our temperature not only through the heat generated by metabolism but in other ways, including clothes, air conditioning and central heating.

Not all dinosaurs necessarily regulated their body temperature in the same way, and some may have done so in ways that are very different from those of any living mammals or reptiles. For many dinosaurs, body temperature probably remained fairly constant,

XXL.—Ideal scene in the Lower Cretaceous Period, with Iguanodon and Megalosaurus.

Illustration showing an iguanodon battling a megalosaurus, from *Gately's World Progress*, ed. C. E. Beale (1886). Ever since dinosaurs were discovered, the public has been fascinated by combats among these titans, which were imagined as very far from sluggish.

simply because their vast size prevented rapid loss of heat. In any case, the new perspective on the abilities of dinosaurs was a good deal less novel than most people realized. The Victorian pictures of dinosaurs by John Martin had shown them as anything but sluggish, as they ceaselessly pounced on and devoured one another. Though he did not seem to realize this, Bakker had actually been advocating the image of dinosaurs shown in most movies and popular literature. Dinosaurs were, in other words, viewed

From *The Iconographic Encyclopedia* (1857). Various reptiles and amphibians, especially the crocodile, are depicted here as relentless predators. Though there is a degree of sensationalism here, crocodiles were, and still are, a frequent threat to people in many parts of the world.

essentially as they had always been, much like the dragons of legend before them.

The debates probably did raise the status of dinosaurs, though not in the way their advocates initially intended. They failed to show that dinosaurs are basically like mammals; they did show that – in order to be lively, interesting and intelligent – dinosaurs did not have to be mammalian.[18] The new research blurred the distinction between warm-blooded and cold-blooded, which traditionally had been a measure of the worth and importance of animals, with greater status going (of course) to the endotherms.

This division goes back at least to Zoroastrianism, according to which the warm-blooded animals were created by Ahura Mazda and the cold-blooded ones were created by Ahriman. That idea was then incorporated into the Abrahamic faiths through the Book of Leviticus, in which, with some exceptions, the warm-blooded animals are 'clean' and the cold-blooded ones are 'unclean'. In later culture, it continued to form a sort of zoological distinction between 'our kind', the animals that resembled human beings, and the 'others'. In the tenth edition of his *Systema naturae* (1758), Linnaeus called animals in the class amphibia, which contained both reptiles and amphibians, 'foul and loathsome'. He added,

> Most amphibians [i.e., exothermic animals] are abhorrent because of their cold body, pale colour, cartilaginous skeleton, filthy skin, fierce aspect, calculating eye, offensive smell, harsh voice, squalid habitation, and terrible venom; and so their Creator has not exerted his powers to make many of them.[19]

To call somebody 'cold-blooded' still usually means that the person is callous, unfeeling and perhaps even a hardened criminal.

The fact is, however, that mammalian predators kill with at least as much gusto as reptilian ones, and with as little indication of remorse. Over the past several decades, people have been learning to regard not only dinosaurs but lizards and other reptiles in more positive ways. Fantastic lizards in popular culture, such as the Silurians in the British television show *Doctor Who*, started to become more human, if not necessarily always more benign.

Jurassic Park by Michael Crichton, first published in 1990, was influenced by the recent debates about dinosaurs, and it alternately glamorizes, pities and criticizes the scientists. As it begins, mysterious lizards appear in Costa Rica, and one of them bites a child. Investigators discover that the animals are actually dinosaurs from a theme park being created on a nearby island by an eccentric billionaire. The dinosaurs have been cloned and so carefully monitored that, initially, the scientists and technicians responsible for the park think it impossible that any dinosaur could have been able to breed or escape. Each is constantly tracked by computer, and all are female. But a mathematician who specializes in chaos theory warns that this desired scenario involved too many variables and, therefore, is inherently unpredictable. It turns out that the DNA used in cloning was extracted from amber and, since complete strands were not available, they were spliced together using DNA from a frog that was capable of changing sex, an ability that it passed on to the dinosaurs, enabling them to breed despite extensive precautions.

Most of the book consists of chase scenes, in which a team of scientists, engineers and officials, accompanied by a couple of children, try to contain and control the dinosaurs, especially those that feed on human flesh. After many people have been killed, the survivors are taken away by helicopter, and the Costa Rican Air Force destroys the dinosaurs on the island with bombs. But it is too late to contain the environmental damage entirely,

Illustration from the graphic novel *Bête Noire* (2012) by Bryan Talbot. From the point of view of the mammals here, reptiles are 'beasts'.

and a herd of feral dinosaurs is already moving through the Costa Rican rainforest.[20]

Whether or not Crichton modelled Jurassic Park after, or even knew about, the Crystal Palace Park, the similarities between the two are remarkable. One apparent difference, apart from technology, between the two theme parks is that the story of Jurassic Park is intended to show the dangerous character of contemporary science, while the Crystal Palace Park was, at least superficially, a grand celebration of the advance of human knowledge. Nevertheless, the imagery of extreme violence that surrounded the early study of dinosaurs suggests that, behind the buoyant optimism that pervaded the Crystal Palace Park, there was some hidden ambivalence. The use of chaos theory to explain the age of dinosaurs in the book seems, despite its postmodern ring, almost Victorian, since thinkers of that era regarded the great reptiles as belonging to an age of turmoil and anarchy.

Both theme parks are placed on islands, making them close to civilization, yet set apart. Both are designed to be enjoyably frightening yet entirely safe. Both blended science, commerce and entertainment, to a point where it was difficult to distinguish among the three. Both were, in some way, intended to reanimate the dragons of remote times, and both employed a great deal of artifice. Perhaps most significantly, both saw the dinosaurs as fierce, as highly active and, in many cases, as insatiable predators, which spend nearly every waking moment hunting or eating. This last point was emphasized even more in Steven Spielberg's blockbuster film *Jurassic Park*, based on the book and released in 1993; it is,

Contemporary painting of the dinosaur Tyrannosaurus rex, together with its smaller, faster cousin Deinonychus. Like most recent depictions, it incorporates new discoveries about dinosaur morphology, such as the revelation that the T-rex, unlike most lizards of today, did not drag its tail, but the vision of unrestrained predation is not so different from that in the work of Benjamin Waterhouse Hawkins and John Martin.

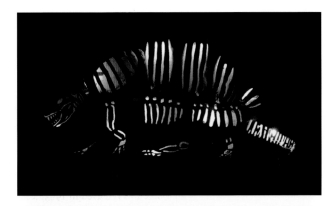

Dinosaur made entirely of lit pumpkins for 'The Great Jack-O-Lantern Blaze', an autumn festival at Van Courtland Manor in Croton-On-Hudson, New York. Dinosaurs have now joined goblins, ghosts and witches as a part of Halloween and other celebrations.

Model of a dinosaur from the movie *Jurassic Park* attacking a car, Museo Nazionale del Cinema, Turin, Italy, *c.* 1993. The monster here is an embodiment of human destructiveness.

essentially, an old-fashioned horror movie with lots of screaming but comparatively little blood and gore.

The film *Jurassic Park* immediately became a lucrative franchise for Universal Pictures. If the first movie was like the Crystal Park Dinosaurs, the successors were more like the dinosaur paintings of John Martin. The first sequel was *The Lost World*, based on a novel by Crichton of the same title and released in 1997.[21] In it, the dinosaurs have been kept in a reconstituted park, where they have been made increasingly large and vicious through genetic engineering, simply to satisfy the public demand for sensationalism. These dragons escape and go on a rampage, in which they incessantly devour one another and human beings until soldiers finally subdue them. It is remarkable how little, in spite of all the scientific discoveries, our images of these giant lizards have changed since Victorian times. The films go back to paradigms that are far older still, for the escaped dinosaurs represent an eruption of primeval chaos, not unlike the children of Tiamat, the creations of Ahriman, the titans of Greek mythology or the dragon of the apocalypse.

Many themes and motifs seem to run through the depiction of giant lizards such as dragons and dinosaurs, regardless of whether they are made in the name of religion, legend or science. Perhaps the boundaries of these activities are far more fluid than people often think. The paradigm of Marduk slaying Tiamat or Saint George killing a dragon was repeated in Crichton's novel, when the Costa Rican Air Force bombs the dinosaurs in Jurassic Park. As Judy Allen and Jeanne Griffiths put it,

> The dragon as Primal Waters, or as Chaos, was often killed as a part of the act of creation, sometimes so that its body could be used to form the structure of an ordered universe, and sometimes because it opposed the act and attempted to sabotage it.[22]

Yet it is quite a paradox that the lizard, which is generally among the most innocuous of animals, should repeatedly become such an object of terror. With very few exceptions, lizards are not venomous, as many snakes are, and they do not overpower people as do tigers and bears. They have never, so far as we know, been carriers of major epidemics, as have mosquitoes or rodents. Yet they conjure images in our imagination that can inspire greater horror than any of those creatures. Perhaps it may be in part their seeming innocence that adapts them to that role, a bit like evil children in horror movies.

Another explanation is that the fear of lizards may be part of our 'collective unconscious', a concept postulated by Carl Gustave Jung. The most famous articulation of this idea comes from scientist Carl Sagan in his best-selling *Dragons of Eden*. He theorized that the fear of dragons was an ancestral inheritance from the time when our evolutionary forefathers encountered enormous reptiles. He was unable to say exactly when or how this happened, but indulged in colourful speculations:

> Could there have been manlike creatures who actually encountered tyrannosaurus rex? Could there have been dinosaurs that escaped the extinctions of the Cretaceous period? Could the pervasive dreams and common fear of 'monsters,' which children develop shortly after they are able to talk, be evolutionary vestiges of quite adaptive – baboonlike – responses to dragons and owls?[23]

The fossil record of lizards is very patchy, but we know that the megalania, a monitor lizard of Australia, reached lengths of up to 6 m (20 ft) or more, about twice that of the largest Komodo dragons, and probably ate human beings. It may have become extinct as recently as 19,000 years ago, which means that there could be a record of it in myths or cave paintings. Fragmentary though Sagan's idea is, we may have no better way to explain why giant lizards so haunt the human imagination.

5 The Lizard in Art

It does not do to leave a live dragon out of your calculations, if you live near him.
J.R.R. Tolkien, *The Hobbit*

If you count dragons (including dinosaurs) as lizards, there are probably more representations of lizards in art around the world than of any other animal. If, however, you do not count dragons, there is a puzzling lack of such representations. Artists have probably been inhibited by a feeling that a picture of a small, realistic lizard might diminish the dragon, a figure that merits respect, whether as a friend or an adversary. This chapter, however, is about what we might call 'realistic' lizards. More specifically, it is about attempts, perhaps never entirely successful, to separate the lizard from the dragon.

Lizards are wonderfully graceful, and so they were often used as decoration on bowls and other artefacts in many Native American cultures. Nevertheless, even in China, Japan and other parts of East Asia, where there is an intense appreciation of smaller creatures such as insects, pictures of lizards (not counting dragons) have never been very common. Whenever somebody began to paint a lizard, it usually turned into a dragon.

Viewed naively, lizards are considered 'creepy-crawlies', together with centipedes, arachnids and snakes. These are animals that some people find 'filthy', yet others consider fascinating. They are often found in remote, neglected places, from arid plains to shady bogs and puddles on the forest floor. Isolation can make their environments appear frightening, even diabolical. These were the sorts of places in which necromancers of legend might summon the Devil or witches would hold their Sabbath.

But creatures in these areas, especially lizards, also give an impression of enormous resilience and fertility. Like snakes, lizards change their skins, though usually shedding the old layer a little at a time, so both could be symbols of resurrection. Both reptiles have a remarkable ability to recover from injuries, and many lizards, as we have seen, even cast off and regenerate their tails. For a few artists and researchers of the late Renaissance and early modern period, these little areas of wilderness contained a divine presence.

In the Bible, God curses the snake for tempting Eve, condemning it to crawl on its belly and to eat dust (Genesis 3:14), but this seems to imply that the animal once had some other form of locomotion. Rabbinical commentaries often ascribed legs and feet to the serpent before the Fall. The snake of Eden was an ambiguous and vaguely delineated figure that did not always fit easily into official versions of Christianity and Judaism, with their relatively sharp divisions between people and animals.

In the late Middle Ages, the serpent in Paradise was often given the head and upper body of a woman, together with a long, scaly tail. At times it has a serpentine body with a human face and arms, and at others it has human legs as well. In some pictures, such as *The Fall of Adam*, painted by the Flemish master Hugo van der Goes in about 1489, the figure is very clearly a lizard. Occasionally it was given some features of a scorpion or locust.

Before about 1100, demons had been modelled primarily on monkeys, and they were mostly black or dark brown. For the following two centuries, the serpent of Eden, known as the 'dracontopede', became a template for increasingly fantastic, reptilian demons. The new style gave these devils many shades of green, blue, red and other vivid colours. Throughout the

Renaissance and early modern period, demons would become increasingly intricate composites. In Italy, the reptilian template gave way to one based on bats and other mammals at around the start of the fourteenth century.

About a century later, artists, led by Signorelli and Michelangelo, painted devils that were almost human, with just a few bestial features such as horns or bat wings to remind us of their diabolical nature. The demons expressed rage through their faces and, above all, their muscular tension.[1] The humanist movement had pervaded Italian culture to a point that man, and not nature, seemed to be the source of evil as well as good.

The diabolic model based on lizards and other reptiles lasted far longer in northern Europe, especially in Germany, Flanders and the Netherlands. Among the many artists who specialized in demons was Martin Schongauer of Germany (*c.* 1440–1491), who took much of his inspiration by going to open markets near to ports and observing the bodies of the creatures that were sold there. He freely combined the fins, heads, limbs and entrails of several animals to create monsters. But, fantastic as these creations were, tapered tails, scales, crests and claws generally seem to mark them as lizards, at least more than any other sort of beast.

In the works of Hieronymus Bosch (*c.* 1455–1516), lizard-like demons proliferate, but the horror they evoke is mixed with fascination, while the artist's unrestrained fantasy is combined with a scientific sort of curiosity. Many of his scenes are set against the background of swamps, which would have been of little interest to artists of previous generations, and they show cycles of growth, decay, predation and renewal. A good example is the painting 'Paradise', the first panel in his famous triptych of *c.* 1501 entitled *The Garden of Earthly Delights*.

All is not well in this paradise. In a circular opening in the fantastic fountain in the centre, an owl, perhaps the demon Lilith, gazes out ominously. Judaeo-Christian tradition had held that animals did not eat one another until after the Great Flood, for how else could they have all got through the journey in Noah's Ark? But in the lower right corner of this painting, a cat is preparing to devour a mouse, while in the lower left, a fantastic lizard is eating a frog or toad, and in the upper left, one mammal, perhaps a bear or lion, is eating another.

In the middle-right side of the painting, a large group of lizards is seen walking up out of the lake to land, possibly seeking the sunlight. One of them has three heads, and another has fanciful armour, but, for the most part, they are realistically painted. From our perspective today, the scene suggests the initial emergence of life from the primordial sea in evolution, and perhaps Bosch even had an intuition of that process.

Martin Schongauer, *The Temptation of St Anthony*, c. 1470. The wildly imaginative monsters here incorporate features of many sorts of animals, but the preponderance of crests, claws and scales probably makes them closer to being lizards than anything else.

Hugo van der Goes, *The Fall of Adam*, late 15th century, left panel of the Vienna diptych. The serpent here is a lizard and, at the same time, a double of Eve.

In the phantasmagoric painting *Mad Meg* (*Dulle Griet*) by Pieter Bruegel the Elder (*c.* 1528–1569), painted in about 1563, the armoured figure of Meg, carrying a sword in her right hand and booty in the left, leads a band of women in pillage to the very jaws of hell. Far to the left is the gaping mouth of the Devil, who has round scales and huge, expressionless eyes. Both figures are surrounded by fantastic creatures. A number of lizards are scattered

Hieronymus Bosch, 'Paradise', left panel from the triptych *The Garden of Earthly Delights*, c. 1501. Note the mostly realistic lizards crawling up from the lake at centre right.

through the picture. As demons pull up a drawbridge to hell, two lizards, which are very true to life, are falling off, and one starts to tumble further into the water. Underneath Meg, in the exact horizontal centre of the painting, is another lizard rearing up in an aggressive posture. The painting was executed at a time when witch trials in Europe were becoming increasingly common, and the nocturnal gathering of wild women suggests a witches' Sabbath. There seems to be a sort of parallel between the lizard and Meg, who appears a little reptilian, with her unnaturally elongated neck, a brownish green dress and a pot sticking out behind her like a tail. It is probably impossible to explain all the symbolism in the picture, but she seems to be a sorceress, while the lizard beside her is a familiar.

It would require the art of natural history to clearly distinguish between the lizard and the dragon. Only in historically recent times has zoology stripped away many imaginative ornaments to reveal the animals we know as 'lizards' today. But we should not forget that science, particularly in its relatively early stages, was driven by religious passion. To learn about the world, especially about natural history, was to reveal more of God's plan. This meant that environments and the creatures that filled them – which had once seemed frightening or insignificant – became worthy of study as creations of God.

An unknown writer – probably in Alexandria – who went under the name of Physiologus or 'physician' wrote in the fourth century that the lizard could regenerate more than just its tail and skin. He reported that the 'sun lizard', probably what we now call a 'wall lizard', eventually lost its sight in old age. It would then find a wall facing eastwards, locate a crack in the wall, and crawl into the opening. When the sun rose again in the east, its eyes would be renewed and open once again. Physiologus concluded,

Pieter Breugel the Elder, *Dulle Griet* (*Mad Meg*), 1562.

Dulle Griet, detail. The two lizards on the right, among the very few realistic animals in the painting, leave Hell as the drawbridge is drawn up, and one falls into the water.

And you, oh man . . . see that, when the eyes of your heart are clouded, you seek . . . Jesus Christ . . . As the Apostle says, 'He is the sun of justice.' He will open for you the intelligible eyes of your heart, and for you the old clothing will become new.[2]

The author did not explain how the lizard could find a wall or a crack without eyesight, but readers were primarily interested in the religious lesson. The parable would constantly be repeated in medieval bestiaries over the next millennium.

The lizard, in consequence, became an attribute of St John the Baptist. Like the reptile, John had lived in the wilderness – in fact, he even survived on 'honey and locusts', the sorts of thing that lizards might eat. As the saint had sought out Christ, the lizard looked for the light. This symbolism would continue in secularized form, giving impetus to the study of natural history. In the early modern period, light, as a manifestation of divine wisdom, was an obsession of scientists such as Newton and poets such as Goethe. It was also a preoccupation of painters from Italy to the Netherlands, and the ways in which many lizards respond to light gave them new attention and respect.

The art of the West had been largely religious since the end of the Roman Empire, and it had been inhibited by the biblical prohibition against 'graven images'. Art of the Byzantine Empire was deliberately unrealistic, and painters often not only merely ignored but deliberately defied rules of perspective. They made figures in the background large, while those in the foreground were small. They also avoided giving the saints or sinners they depicted facial expressions on the grounds that they were painting them not in a temporal perspective but in that of eternity. Landscapes were suggested, but not depicted in detail. The Islamic and Jewish artists often went further, avoiding figurative art altogether, and producing instead intricate organic and geometric designs.

The traditional painting of China, Japan and other parts of East Asia had been more devoted to careful observation, and this gradually made its way westwards. When the Muslim Mughals conquered much of India in the seventeenth century, they fostered a style that combined the clean lines of traditional Islamic art with the Hindu regard for animals. The early Mughal emperors, including Babur, Akbar and Jahangir, loved the natural world and enthusiastically patronized the arts. Their subjects produced many beautifully detailed paintings of flowers, birds, insects and other animals, some of which would later be taken to England and continental Europe, especially in the era of the British Empire. But lizards were surprisingly rare even in the paintings of the East Asian, Indian and Near Eastern artists, probably because they still evoked strong associations with dragons.

In the West, the margins of illuminated manuscripts of the later Middle Ages and Renaissance provided a free space in which artists could indulge their inclinations without being bound by elaborate religious or secular conventions. Painters could, according to preference, be as fantastic, realistic, lyrical or comical as they liked. In books of hours from the later Middle Ages and Renaissance, this resulted in many of the most unrestrained fantasies ever depicted. Heads and torsos of both people and animals were shown emerging out of the stems of plants. Rabbits strung up vanquished hunters by the feet as game, and knights in armour faced off against gigantic snails. Centaurs were shown aiming arrows at faces that emerged out of their long tails. But the margins of manuscripts also contained highly detailed, realistic depictions of small creatures that were unprecedented in Western art. The foundation of these pictures was mostly flowers and other vegetation, arranged in symmetrical patterns. With the flowers came insects,

Dulle Griet, detail. The lizard just beneath Mad Meg seems to mimic her posture, and it is probably her familiar.

drawn with the same concern for realistic detail, including butterflies, moths and dragonflies, and occasionally lizards.

The Renaissance was a period of globalization, in which ships brought back from distant lands not only ideas and wealth but dried plants, animal skins, skeletons, botanical illustrations and all manner of curiosities, which filled the cabinets of rulers such as the Holy Roman Emperor Rudolf II (*r.* 1583–1612) and, on a slightly smaller scale, countless aristocratic houses. These inspired artists to observe individual examples of fauna and flora more closely, yet it also detached them from their natural context. There was still, at most, only an incipient understanding of the intricate ways in which living things interact in a natural environment. The result was often paintings and illustrations that were extremely precise in detail, yet highly imaginative in their arrangement. As artists became increasingly fascinated by the way in which sunlight passes through petals and is reflected by water, they paid more attention to lizards, which are sensitive to light.

The French ceramicist Bernard Palissy (c. 1510–1590) took the dragon out of the lizard and the Devil out of the snake. He developed a new technique that made major distortions almost impossible. As an amateur scientist, he was among the first people to recognize correctly how fossils were created, and that insight influenced his art. He would take a pewter plate and arrange dead leaves, shells and other objects from the forest floor on it, and he would press them against the surface. He would place lizards, snakes, frogs, fish and perhaps other small creatures

Kitagawa Utamaro, woodblock print of a snake and lizard, 1788. The organic lines of the two reptiles blend with those of the vegetation, and even the calligraphy. Utamaro has written in the upper right, 'I am sending you a long, wistful letter written on paper rolled up like a coiled snake . . .'

Painting of a chameleon by Mughal artist Ustad Mansur, early 17th century. The clear lines, bright colours and careful observation are characteristic of Mughal artists.

on it, and make a clay mould of the entire composition, which would afterwards be used to construct a ceramic plate or bowl. He would add a few details by hand, such as the currents of flowing water, and then paint the scene, primarily in shades of brown, green and blue. Finally, he would fire the piece, producing a soft, translucent glaze.[3] He called the style 'rustic ware', and also made mugs, pitchers and other objects. Such creations were, in effect, artificial fossils.

This approach was scientific, but it was not entirely secular. He viewed fossils as analogous to the 'philosopher's stone' sought by alchemists, and making them was a way of imitating the work of God. His ceramics would not transmute base metals into gold, but it would transfigure the fragile bodies of leaves, lizards or frogs into a permanent form.[4] Palissy was a devoutly religious Huguenot who would eventually die imprisoned in the Bastille rather than renounce his faith. He felt personally drawn to the sort of hidden corners that many contemporaries would have considered desolate, but his purpose was to reveal that the presence of God was to be found even there. It was to demonstrate that, far from being just a primeval chaos, the unfrequented woodlands and swamps were actually places of order.

This is shown by the symmetry of his compositions. Very often, there is a small island, surrounded by water, depicted in the middle of the plate. On the island is a large lizard or snake, surrounded by smaller creatures. There may be a few fish and crustaceans in the

Maria Sibylla Merian, branch of a cassava with black tegu or lizard and white peacock butterfly, illustration to *Metamorphosis insectorum Surinamensium (Insects of Suriname)*, Dutch edition (1719). Careful observation here has managed to separate the lizard from the dragon, its fanciful relative, yet perhaps not entirely.

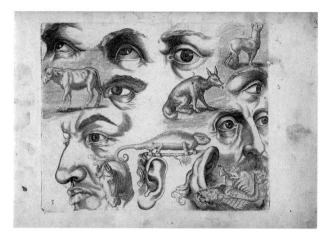

'Eyes' by Michael Synders, 1610. Emerging theories of physiognomy maintained that the character of a person could be ascertained by the resemblance of his/her features to those of animals.

water. Along the banks opposite the island are other lizards, frogs and snakes, arranged in fairly symmetrical patterns. The animals themselves often form geometric arrangements – for example, the snakes may be coiled in a circle, and the bodies of the lizards form an undulating curve. For Palissy, the reptiles, amphibians, insects and crustaceans around a woodland pond were a sort of community, which, in many ways, might parallel that of human society, with its cultures, classes and professions.

In Palissy's time, ceramic techniques were secrets that were generally closely guarded from rival workshops, and Palissy took his methods to the grave. In the first half of the nineteenth century, Charles-Jean Avisseau of Tours (1796–1861) rediscovered Palissy's techniques, using the same laborious process of trial and error as the man who had created them. An exhibit of Avisseau's pottery was featured prominently at the Crystal Palace exhibition in London in 1851, and it inspired a European vogue for creating works of 'Palissy Ware', in which lizards were very often depicted, during the later nineteenth century.[5]

Unlike Palissy, Avisseau sculpted the creatures in his work, rather than using moulds. His home was full of many varieties of lizards, along with other creatures. While Palissy had been a man of the Renaissance who was intrigued by the play of water, light and air, Avisseau shared with other European Romantics the fascination with the sombre forest. His palette is darker than Palissy's, and his compositions are far more densely packed. Theories of evolution from Lamarck to Darwin gave the swamps and woods a new significance, as perhaps a cradle of early terrestrial life, and Avisseau, together with the other creators of Palissy Ware, celebrated their primeval fertility. Palissy and Avisseau did not take the dragon out of the lizard. They placed both creatures in a realm that was safe from marauding knights.

In seventeenth-century Flanders and the Netherlands, flower painting probably still carried a hint of frivolity, and it certainly had less prestige than mythological or overtly religious subjects. Nevertheless, pictures of flowers far outsold everything else among the emerging middle classes.[6] The flowers in a vase were at once a celebration of growing affluence and – since they would not live long – a reminder of the transience of earthly things. Light was associated with God and darkness with the Devil, and the play of shadows suggested an eternal struggle between the two.

For artists such as Roelant Savery (1576–1639) from Flanders and Balthasar van der Ast (1593–1657) from the Netherlands, the flowers became the centre of a natural community. The flowers attracted insects, which in turn brought reptiles and amphibians that preyed on them, all of which participated in a cycle of birth, growth, decay and death. Cut and placed in a vase with water, flowers suggested domestication of the natural world, with all the pleasures, labours and uncertainties that entailed. The cold-blooded creatures they attracted suggested the resilience of the

Bowl from the workshop of Bernard Palissy, later 16th century. Palissy found order, symmetry and beauty in environments that most of his contemporaries considered savage and chaotic.

Plate attributed to Bernard Palissy, mid-16th century. Unlike the 19th-century ceramicists who were influenced by his work, Palissy did not emphasize predation. Here the lizard and snake, instead of facing off against one another, as was conventional, are turned in varied directions.

Otto Marseus van Schrieck, *The Forest Floor with a Snake, Lizards, Butterflies and other Insects*, 1650–78. The butterflies and the snake are solitary, while the lizards are social.

Balthasar van der Ast, *Still-life of Flowers, Fruit, Shells, and Insects*, c. 1629. In the 17th and 18th centuries, the 's' curve was often considered the most graceful of patterns, and the lizard on the left exemplifies it perfectly.

natural world, which followed the blossoms, and placed the entire enterprise of domestication in question.

Flies, attracted by dying blooms, represented rot, while butterflies, attracted by fresh ones, symbolized resurrection. Snakes or toads, at the base of the bouquet, might call to mind the Devil. The most ambivalent, and, thereby most interesting, of the creatures would be lizards. As creatures that seek the light, they might represent eternal life, and they often seemed to be guarding the flowers from noxious pests. A lizard hungrily eyeing a butterfly could suggest a demon coveting a human soul, while one preying on flies might come across as a guardian angel.

Otto Marseus van Shrieck (1613–1678), who shared the fascination of earlier artists such as Bosch and Palissy with wastelands, developed a new genre known as 'forest floor painting'. He painted flowers not cut and arranged in vases but growing in forbidding corners of the woods, surrounded by ferns, toadstools and obscure types of vegetation. These were grouped with reptiles and

insects from various regions, which he knew largely through curio cabinets and natural history books, arranged in artificial poses and combinations for dramatic effect. Van Schrieck emphasized predation and endowed reptiles with a special ferocity. They were often depicted lunging at prey, with their mouths open wide.

He retained many conventions of earlier flower painting, but made the scenes he painted into a sort of savage Eden, not altogether unlike that of Bosch. He endowed his subjects with allegorical meaning, perhaps anticipating the comparison of the unconscious mind with a forest made by later psychologists such as C. G. Jung. The blossoming plant in the centre of a canvas suggested the Tree of Knowledge, while the flowers were a tempting fruit, and a lizard at the base gazed upwards with a human sort of intensity, waiting for Adam and Eve to set foot in its domain. This was an early expression of the Romantic longing for wildness that would grow steadily as industrialization progressed. There was a huge vogue for such paintings in the second half of the seventeenth century, and van Schrieck was widely imitated.[7]

Rachel Ruysch (1664–1750) began her career under the influence of van Schrieck and sometimes painted scenes of the forest floor, but eventually turned to more conventional floral arrangements. Like van Schrieck, she depicted dark backgrounds, asymmetrical arrangements and lizards in the shadows. She was far less interested, however, in dramatic confrontations of predator with prey than in delicate nuances of texture, colour and form.[8] Her lizards seem to be drawn to the tableau not so much out of appetite as by the love of light and colour, in a way that seems almost human.

All of these paintings are pervaded by tension between nature, represented by the flora and fauna, and civilization, represented in most cases by the setting. In his painting *Boy Bitten by a Lizard*, from about 1593, Michelangelo Merisi da Caravaggio (1571–1610),

Rachel Ruysch, *Still-life with Fruit and a Lizard,* c. 1710. The lizard and butterfly here may be small, but they are the most dynamic part of the picture, in which all else is stationary.

with perhaps a touch of satire, makes this conflict relatively explicit. The objects on the table are among those that predominate in European, especially Dutch and Flemish, still-life paintings – a flower in a vase, fruits and a lizard. Like those artists of northern Europe, Caravaggio has clearly taken great trouble to render the play of light around forms and textures. The boy, who is chubby and has a flower in his hair, appears pampered and decadent, perhaps in consequence of the domestic comfort that the painters

Michelangelo Merisi da Caravaggio, *Boy Bitten by a Lizard*, c. 1593. The lizard here is an embodiment of nature, resisting domestication by the decadent young man.

of those scenes often celebrated. The lizard has just bitten the young man, who recoils in pain – the revenge of the natural world.

It was not the teeth and claws of lizards that inspired fear, but rather the feeling that lizards belonged to a primordial world. In East Asia, this was celebrated as a source of cosmic energy. In the West, particularly in the early modern and Victorian periods, it was a world of unrestrained predation, a state of savagery from which we had emerged with great difficulty, and to which we might easily return. This terror of reversion has returned whenever a serious attempt is made to represent lizards in a realistic way, from the gloomy paradise of Bosch to the forest floor of Otto van Schrieck and the primeval seas of John Martin.

As the woods of northwestern Europe were cut down or placed under more extensive management, and the swamps were drained, lizards probably became rarer. Perhaps a vase of flowers left outside in Flanders or the Netherlands would at one time have really attracted lizards, as they seem to in paintings of the sixteenth and seventeenth centuries, but that is no longer the case. The population density of lizards is relatively hard to estimate even today, since they are generally solitary and inconspicuous, and they are dispersed over wide areas.[9]

To some extent, the Victorian fairy painters may have inherited the traditions of artists like Van Schrieck, since they shared with them a fascination with obscure places in the woods – filled with fungi, ferns, insects and reptiles – but such settings had lost a lot of their wildness by the nineteenth century. Rather than reminders of a primeval world, these became the places where diminutive fairies and elves held nightly revels. In crowded, highly urbanized countries, it was hard to find places where supernatural beings might reside, unless they lived on a diminutive scale. The reduction in size also reflected the association of both folkloric figures and animals with children in popular culture. The smallness of these figures made even ordinary lizards appear to be dragons. In *The Fairies*, an illustration to Shakespeare's play *A Midsummer Night's Dream* by Gustave Doré of 1873, pixies are using lizards as mounts.

J. J. Grandville (a pseudonym for Jean Ignace Isidore Gérard, 1803–1847) made engravings of satirical fantasies in which the protagonists often blended human and bestial features. Were these anthropomorphized animals or bestialized men and women? It is impossible to say. But even tigers and bison seemed a little too 'human' for Grandville, and he was at his best drawing grasshoppers in military uniforms or crocodiles seated around the banquet table. In the last year of his life, he produced, in collaboration with writer Alphonse Karr, a book entitled *Les Fleurs animées* (The Animated Flowers), in which the biting satire of his earlier work gave way to a more lyrical kind of humour. Women are pictured as flowers, while the men are reptiles and insects, who may surround them in adoration or offend them with vulgarity, yet cannot enter their realm. In the picture of the narcissus, for example, a white flower with a woman's face contemplates her reflection in the water, while, unnoticed, a lizard gazes up pleadingly at her.

J. J. Grandville, 'Narcisses', illustration to *Fleurs animées* (1867). The fairies have returned to earth in the form of flowers, while the lizards and insects represent men.

After the styles of realistic still-life painting and Palissy Ware had run their course, lizards were never again incorporated into artistic conventions. They were used most often as designs for jewellery, but also appeared occasionally on housewares, leather goods and textiles. But in the twentieth century, lizards, even including dragons, did not often appear in Western art.

The emphasis in art shifted increasingly from rural to urban settings. The Impressionists may have painted landscapes, but leading figures such as Claude Monet, Pierre-Auguste Renoir and Camille Pissarro specialized in highly cultivated ones such as public parks, orchards and gardens. The Dadaists, Futurists and Cubists were fascinated by the rhythms of machines. Artists in general were preoccupied with social messages or individual sensibility, rather than with the natural world. When two world wars of unprecedented destructiveness broke out and traditions disintegrated, many people felt that focusing on flora and fauna was escapist.

Gustave Doré, *The Fairies*, 1873. Among the little people, everything is on a smaller scale, and the lizard directly in the centre of the picture serves as a mount.

An exception was the German Expressionist Franz Marc (1880–1914), who was increasingly obsessed with animals towards the end of his life. He painted them using colours and lines that might seem 'unrealistic', not simply to stylize their appearance, but in recognition of the fact that they perceived the world using senses very different from our own. While other artists endeavoured to render human subjectivity, he tried to paint the world

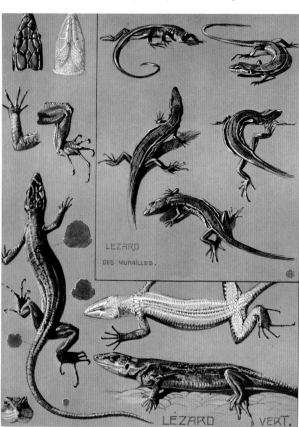

Illustration showing green and wall lizards by Mathurin Méheut from *Études d'animaux* (c. 1920). Méheut was a Breton painter who generally kept aloof from the fashions of his time, and concentrated on seascapes and animals. This study shows a particular fascination with the way lizards coordinate their limbs and tails while in motion.

154

Illustration to *Das Thier in der decorativen Kunst* by Anton Seder (1896). Artists in the styles of Jugendstil and Art Nouveau – whose work appeared largely in picture books, posters and public places – were drawn to the organic, curvilinear lines of lizards.

as it might be seen by a horse or a fox, even when that might not make sense to men and women. In his woodcut entitled *Lizards* of 1912, Marc uses the sinuous forms of lizards to create patterns that are close to abstraction.

As we, at the beginning of the twenty-first century, face the prospect of ecological catastrophe, animals and plants in art seem very far from being an indulgence. Artists, however, have still not yet rediscovered the supple grace of lizards. In popular culture, as we have seen, dinosaurs are roused from the depths, as in *Godzilla*, or resurrected, as in *Jurassic Park*. Perhaps, in an analogous way, lizards hibernate in our unconscious, to be roused by cataclysms to come.

6 Lizards Today

The lizard that lives high up in iroko tree does not hear the lions roar.
Proverb of Botswana

When I first visited the Westchester County, New York, Reptile Exposition in early 2015, I was startled to see two queues at the entrance that extended around the block. The huge exhibition hall was packed, and children, especially, paid rapt attention to lizards of just about every size and colour. Nearly half of the items sold at the reptile fair, particularly those pertaining to lizards, were about entertainment rather than practical care. Many of the vendors sold DVDs of movies featuring cinematic lizards such as Godzilla. There were quite a few models of the lizard-like characters from the *Star Wars* movies, *Doctor Who* and other works of fantasy or science fiction. Other booths offered tattoos and dolls of both real and imaginary lizards.

For the many children at the Westchester County Exposition, lizards are dragons, perhaps baby dragons. An advantage of such fantasy is that it can lead to a greater appreciation of lizards, and perhaps aid efforts on behalf of their conservation. A disadvantage is that it may lead people to neglect practicalities, for example by buying a lizard that they lack the knowledge and resources to care for properly. Fantasy can lead us to real lizards, or else distract us away from them. Contact with lizards and amphibians, even when sporadic, doubtless nourishes the dragons of our imagination, which otherwise might become overly stereotyped and formulaic.

Ultimately, this is simply part of the human relationship with lizards, and probably neither good nor bad. We have very distinctive parameters for our relationships with different animals, especially domestic ones. These involve different permissions, duties, expectations, needs and so on, and these are very difficult, even for scholars of human–animal relations, to explain. Why do we eat pigs but not dogs in the West today? Why are shepherds so fiercely protective of their sheep, which they themselves will send to slaughter eventually? Why are Westerners, unlike Asians and Africans, so intolerant of feral dogs? A good deal is written on such subjects, but the answers to such questions seldom or never seem complete.

These relationships are determined by traditions, which are formed and modified by interaction between human beings and animals over the centuries. They vary greatly among cultures, and are in constant – and now rapid – evolution. Contemporary pet-keeping, in which animals generally provide people with no service except companionship, is largely a modern, Western phenomenon. So, to a large extent, is our conventional division of animals into pets, livestock, working animals and wild creatures.

Mosaic in the 81st Street metro station in New York City, next to the American Museum of Natural History. An iguana and a chameleon are perched over a sign announcing the station. Lizards are far more prominent in public and popular art than in high culture.

But, looking back over the centuries, certain themes in each relationship usually stand out. We look to dogs, for example, to provide emotional companionship. Many people find the directness with which dogs seem to express their feelings refreshing, compared to the reticence, duplicity and pretense that fills interaction among human beings. As with pagan deities or Catholic saints, we tend to associate different animals with particular aspects of our lives: dogs with feelings, cats with domesticity, deer with wildness and birds with freedom.

The cultural history of lizards is also, to a great extent, the story of human creativity. If human culture were an ecosystem, the lizard would be the 'indicator species'. Just as the number of butterflies in a field tells us about an environment, so images of lizards provide information about our civilization.

Though still far behind dogs, cats and birds in popularity, lizards and other reptiles are the most rapidly growing portion of the pet industry in Europe and North America. Part of the reason why people keep lizards as pets is the lure of the exotic. These companions make people think of rainforests and deserts, and have a great range of colours, ornaments and textures. Dogs and cats can seem drab by comparison. But, like all pets, lizards require consistent attentiveness, and their human companions must pay very careful attention to factors such as humidity, heat, space, light and food. Their human companions must periodically examine lizards for any sign of swelling, parasites, sores or other irregularities. The love of esoterica, which attracts people to lizards, can also be dangerously seductive, since it can lead people to adopt ever more unusual species that are not easy to care for. They do not make the same emotional demands on us as dogs or cats, but do they offer the same rewards?

The appeal of lizards as pets does not seem as self-evident as that of warm-blooded animals. Can lizards return human affection?

Monitors and a few teiids respond to petting and stroking, but most lizards do not, yet the apparent lack of reciprocation does not necessarily inhibit many people from holding and embracing them. Herpetologists may be sceptical about whether most reptiles can feel a more human sort of fondness for their caretakers, but many pet owners insist they can, and there is no way to know for sure.

Much of the allure of pets is that they can put us in touch with dimensions of experience far beyond the human world, but dogs may be losing that ability. Just about all of the paraphernalia of human lives in affluent sectors of society have now been extended to dogs, which have their own psychotherapists, designer clothes, antidepressant drugs, jewellery, television channels, gourmet foods and hotels. Dogs are no longer often allowed to run free or kept in separate structures. They share the lives and dwellings of human beings, and are socialized to human society through extensive training. Cats, which have long been considered only partially domesticated, remain less entirely integrated into the patterns of post-industrial society, but their lives are less autonomous than they were a few generations ago. People occasionally dress even lizards in leather jackets and felt hats, but these creatures still seem nevertheless to belong unequivocally to a world that is different from ours.

Vinciane Despret and Temple Grandin have pointed out that, though we usually think of 'empathy' in terms of emotion, it can also be participation in 'a visual community of sensibility'. This is a sort of sympathy that is not based on pathos.[1] It is, in fact, only since the Romantic era of the late eighteenth and nineteenth centuries that we have thought of personal identity primarily as a matter of feelings. I do not doubt at all that lizards, and other cold-blooded creatures, are capable of many basic emotions such as anger or fear. I suspect, however, that emotions detached from any

At the Westchester, New York, reptile exposition, a vendor shows off an Australian bearded dragon that clings to her shirt.

Do lizards feel affection for people? This visitor to the Westchester County Reptile Exposition holds a panther chameleon, native to Madagascar. It has wrapped itself around her hand, but perhaps the chameleon just thinks she is a tree. One eye, at least, is looking away from her.

apparent object are primarily a human phenomenon. The emotions of lizards may be integrated into their sensuous discernment, to a point where even the distinction between feeling and perception becomes questionable or meaningless. We think of emotion as something 'internal', while what we see is, so to speak, 'out there'. For lizards and other reptiles, there may be little or no distinction between the objective and subjective realms. They encounter events in a manner that is more holistic, and we can experience that as well as through empathy with them. Perhaps, then, the reason why dinosaurs have been consistently associated with lizards may be that those scaly little creatures link us with a primeval world. To the extent that we manage to see through the eyes of a lizard, we enter a sort of Jurassic Park.

We are now entering the sixth great extinction. Environmental scientists estimate that in the next several decades a quarter of all mammals, a fifth of reptiles and a sixth of birds will soon vanish from the earth.[2] Major factors contributing to this include habitat destruction, climate change, the globalization of fauna, toxic chemicals and overexploitation. The process is taking place on such a vast scale that it is difficult even to speak of the fate of one type of animal, whether lizard or human being, in isolation from all the rest.

But I will attempt that for a moment here, even at the risk of sounding 'lizard-centric'. The fate of lizards during this catastrophe is especially complex and difficult to predict. It is possible that the lack of dramatic signals may be leading people to underestimate the crisis faced by lizards. They tend to be spread out over large but thinly populated areas, and are generally solitary, all of which makes it difficult to estimate their populations.[3] Even a relatively rapid decline might initially escape human attention.

On the other hand, global warming might work in favour of lizards, since they tend to thrive in more tropical environments. David Attenborough writes:

the reptiles, the first large animals to colonize dry land, being so efficient and economical in their exploitation of sources of energy needed to do so, seem likely to be extending their empires in the world that is coming.[4]

Even as many species of lizard perish, it is easily possible that others might obtain greatly increased ranges. They may eventually diversify and – who knows? – in time, perhaps after human extinction, even create another 'Age of Dinosaurs'. The fifth great extinction that killed off the dinosaurs, largely precipitated by a huge asteroid that landed in the Gulf of Mexico about 66 million years ago, may turn out to have been just an interruption of an enduring order. The future of lizards, at any rate, is not entirely dependent on human beings, and that realization may inspire alarm, perplexity or relief.

With the pet trade has come a redistribution of wildlife. In the 1970s, Jackson's chameleon, a three-horned lizard from East Africa, was introduced to Hawaii through the pet trade and quickly naturalized. The green iguana, indigenous to Latin America and the Caribbean, has become feral in Hawaii, Florida and Louisiana, abandoned by pet keepers who were not prepared when their companion animals started to approach 1–1.5 m (4–5 ft) in length. Wall lizards from southern Europe, often escaped from pet shops or homes, are thriving in several communities of the American Northeast, as well as in parts of Britain and Canada. Nile monitors, indigenous to most of Africa, have made a home in Catalonia, Spain. The invaders may carry salmonella, spread invasive plants and compete with indigenous wildlife, but the full ecological impact of the introduced species will only be revealed over many decades to come.

Needless to say, lizard populations have also been hurt by the introduction of invasive species. At the end of the Second World

War, the brown tree snake, a native of Australia, was inadvertently introduced to Guam. In addition to causing the extinction of several species of native birds, it devastated the indigenous population of skinks and geckos. The globalization of wildlife, however, has progressed to a point where environmentalists seldom even think of reversing it, but only try to limit the negative impacts.

Debates on how to respond to the globalization of wildlife are often daunting in their complexity. They have a special emotional intensity because of the almost uncanny way in which they mirror controversies about human immigration. A great many subjective associations, of which the debaters are barely conscious, enter into the ecological debates. Some invasive species in the United States such as starlings seem never to be accepted as part of native landscapes even after well over a hundred years, while others, such as English sparrows, though once bitterly resented, are now taken for granted as natural residents. But lizards have an exceptional ability to fit harmoniously into many environments to a point where they cease to be conspicuous, and it seems likely that many will adapt well to their new locations.

But let us again switch from a lizard-centric perspective to a more anthropocentric one. What do lizards do for human beings? On a directly practical level, lizards, like all fauna and flora, are a source of medical and scientific knowledge. We might, for example, learn something about immunities from the Komodo dragon, which can tolerate over fifty strains of bacteria in its saliva. The most obvious use of lizards is in controlling insects, which can spread diseases and threaten crops. This service may begin to seem more dramatic if, as some environmental scientists have predicted, global warming creates a massive proliferation of insects.

But there are good reasons to take some of the services of lizards on faith. Both lizards and human beings are involved in enormously intricate matrices of relationships among living

Adam Elsheimer, *Ceres turning Stellio into a Lizard*, 1605–7. According to Ovid, Ceres, the Roman goddess of grain, changed the young man Stellio into a lizard, for mocking the alacrity with which she ate. 'Stellio' became one of many terms for 'lizard'. Such tales of transformation address our perpetual curiosity about how other creatures see the world.

things that make up the environment. They are far too complex to be described in anything approaching full detail, but that need not prevent us from taking account of our interdependence with other species. Yet perhaps most importantly, images of lizards, in forms such as dragons and dinosaurs, pervade global culture so completely that perhaps we could even not be truly 'human' without them.

Much of the fascination, and also the challenge, of writing about animals is that they place in question all of the categories with which we habitually try to make sense of the world. Our language developed mostly for communication among human beings, and it begins to break down when we try to describe the perceptual realms of other creatures. Our only chance is to speak metaphorically and make unabashed use of our imaginations.

Lizards, like human beings and other living things, exist on several levels. They are part of the endless circulation of organic matter and energy, the body of Mother Earth. They are also a part of a local ecosystem, as well as of communities defined by biological kinship. Human beings, at least in Western culture, usually feel we are defined by the narrower categories. We place a great deal of emphasis on individuality, as well as on ethnicity. For lizards, the more comprehensive categories may be more important. They are, in a sense, more philosophical than human beings.

We human beings constantly feel separated from the natural world, a sentiment that we may call 'exceptionalism' when we feel proud, or 'alienation' when we feel sad. We are extremely prone to individual vanity and a collective self-absorption, but a lizard is often so profoundly integrated into its environment that it can

Wall lizard photographed around Cincinnati, Ohio, in 2012. The lizards from the Mediterranean are now so well established in parts of the American Midwest that, despite being an invasive species, they are protected by law.

seem to be almost without a self. Lizards even take on the colours that surround them, and they are sensually attuned to every motion or change in their vicinity. They lie so still that they can almost be mistaken for vegetation, yet they can react instantaneously if an insect comes in range. Lizards are a great many things that we are not, and that is why they fascinate us.

Human beings traditionally have taken pride in our intellects, but now we externalize our intelligence through the use of computers, mobile phones and countless 'smart' devices. In some respects, these may make us more powerful. Nevertheless, the technological devices limit our autonomy in many ways, since they are involved in, or even make, our decisions, often without our even being aware of it. They suggest Facebook friends, send us subtly customized advertisements and decide what websites will pop up first in an Internet search. Perhaps we are becoming more like lizards, whose intelligence has always been as much in their senses as in their minds. They are alert to any alteration in their surroundings, and respond quickly to changes in scent, motions, temperature and light.

We have now looked at the lizard in many aspects, among others as a sensual being, a symbol, a myth, an evolutionary moment and an aesthetic form. Once again, we must ask, 'What is a lizard?' While the exact significance of the term will inevitably be determined by context, it will always carry at least a wealth of associations. Most of twentieth- and twenty-first-century philosophy, from positivism to deconstruction, has centred on the intensive interrogation of words, but, like the lizard itself, language will always remain something of a mystery. In most circumstances, it may be best just to say, 'A lizard is a lizard.' To use the word in a relatively naive way, with no more qualification than the situation requires, is to affirm sensuous immediacy, tradition and a sense of wonder.

Timeline of Lizards

_c._ 310–320 million years ago

Archosaurs diverge in evolution from lepidosaurs. The former will eventually include birds and crocodilians, while the latter will include most reptiles, excluding turtles but including lizards and snakes

_c._ 135 million years ago

The breaking apart of the supercontinent Pangaea is completed, leaving varieties of lizards geographically separated from one another

66 million years ago

The Cretaceous Extinction destroys three-quarters of extant species, including all non-avian dinosaurs and the giant marine lizards such as mosasaurs and plesiosaurs. Surviving animals including lizards begin to diversify dramatically in order to fill the vacated ecological niches

1515–47

Francis I, known as the 'father of French culture', becomes obsessed with the 'salamander', a mythic lizard that was said to be made of pure fire

_c._ 1555

Ceramicist Bernard Palissy develops the techniques for 'rustic ware', a style of porcelain in which lizards are very prominently depicted

1825

French biologist Pierre André Latreille makes, for the first time, a sharp distinction between reptiles and amphibians. As a result, salamanders and related animals gradually cease to be considered lizards

1854

The Crystal Palace Park opens in London, with sculptures of the giant creatures of the past, based largely on contemporary lizards

c. 2000 BCE

The figure of the mushussu, which resembles a monitor lizard, becomes prominent in the art of Mesopotamia

c. 1046–256 BCE (Chou dynasty)

The yellow dragon with five claws becomes the symbol of the Chinese emperor

c. 400

A Greek writer in Alexandria, Egypt, who goes by the name of 'Physiologus', reports that aged lizards renew their youth by gazing directly at the sun

c. 1600–1750

Dutch artists such as Otto Marseus van Schrieck and Rachel Ruysch feature lizards prominently in paintings of the forest floor and of bouquets of flowers

c. 1703

Father Francisco Ximénez transcribes the Quiché Maya creation epic *Popol Vuh*, which tells of the creation of the world by Qucomatz, a version of the deity known as the 'feathered serpent'

1822

Mary Ann Mantell discovers the bones of a giant creature in Sussex, UK. Her husband, Gideon Mantell, names it 'iguanodon' and describes it as a huge iguana

1954

Toho Studios in Tokyo releases the film *Godzilla*, which is a huge commercial success, and provides the major model for many subsequent horror movies about giant lizards and dinosaurs

c. 1965–85

John Ostrum and other scientists confirm an old theory that birds are descended from dinosaurs. This helps inspire renewed interest in palaeontology

c. 2000

The sixth great extinction in earth's history is under way, and lizards, like all animals, face an uncertain future

References

1 WHAT IS A LIZARD?

1 Shlomo Pesach Toperoff, *The Animal Kingdom in Jewish Thought* (London, 1995), p. 151.
2 Richard Barber, *Bestiary* (Woodridge, 1993), p. 193.
3 Edward Topsell and Thomas Muffet, *The History of Four-footed Beasts and Serpents and Insects* [1658], 3 vols, facs. edn (New York, 1967), vol. II, pp. 613, 737.
4 Oliver Goldsmith, *History of Animated Nature* [1774] (Cheapside, 1838), vol. IV, p. 221.
5 Mary Douglas, *Purity and Danger: An Analysis of Concepts of Pollution and Taboo* [1966] (London, 2003), p. 96.
6 Gregory Forth, 'Symbolic Lizards: Forms of Special Purpose Classification of Animals among the Nage of Eastern Indonesia', *Anthrozoös*, XXVI/3 (Cambridge, 2013), p. 369.
7 Herman Melville, *Moby Dick, or The Whale* [1851] (New York, 1902), pp. 114–17.
8 Thomas Pennant, *History of Quadrupeds*, 2 vols (London, 1793), vol. II, p. 252.
9 Harriet Ritvo, *The Platypus and the Mermaid, and Other Figments of the Classifying Imagination* (Cambridge, MA, 1997), pp. 26–50.
10 S. G. Goodrich, *Johnson's Natural History*, 2 vols (New York, 1859, 1867), vol. II, p. 407.
11 Brent Berlin, *Ethnobiological Classification: Principles of Classification of Plants and Animals in Traditional Societies* (Princeton, NJ, 1992), pp. 3–35.

12 Carol Kaesuk Yoon, *Naming Nature: The Clash between Instinct and Science* (New York, 2009), pp. 191–212.

13 Brent Berlin, 'The First Congress of Ethnozoological Nomenclature', *Journal of the Royal Anthropological Institute*, XII/1 (London, 2006), pp. 23–44.

2 THE DIVERSITY OF LIZARDS

1 Eric R. Pianka and Laurie J. Vitt, *Lizards: Windows to the Evolution of Diversity* (Oakland, CA, 2003), p. 270.

2 Ibid., p. 274.

3 Marty Crump, *Eye of Newt and Toe of Frog, Adder's Fork and Lizard's Leg: The Lore and Mythology of Amphibians and Reptiles* (Chicago, IL, 2015), p. 273.

4 Carl Sagan, *Dragons of Eden: Speculations on the Evolution of Human Intelligence* (New York, 1977), pp. 55–6.

5 Emily Anthes, 'Coldblooded Does Not Mean Stupid', *New York Times* (13 November 2013), p. D1.

6 Walter Burkert, *Creation of the Sacred: Tracks of Biology in Early Religions* (Cambridge, MA, 1966), pp. 35–55.

7 Jérémie Teyssier, Suzanne V. Saenko, Dirk van der Marel and Michel C. Milinkovitch, 'Photonic Crystals Cause Active Colour Change in Chameleons', *Nature Communications*, 6 (March 2015), www.nature.com, accessed 2 December 2015.

3 LIZARDS AND DRAGONS

1 Gregory Forth, 'Symbolic Lizards: Forms of Special Purpose Classification of Animals among the Nage of Eastern Indonesia', *Anthrozoös*, XXVI/3 (Cambridge, 2013), pp. 360–66.

2 Harold Gebhard and Maria Ludwig, *Von Drachen, Yetis, und Vampiren: Fabeltieren auf der Spur* (Munich, 2005), p. 47.

3 Roel Sterckx, *The Animal and Demon in Early Modern China* (Albany, NY, 2002), p. 287.

4 Ray Desmond, *Wonders of Creation: Natural History Drawings in the British Library* (London, 1986), p. 126.

5 Edward Topsell and Thomas Muffet, *The History of Four-footed Beasts and Serpents and Insects* [1658], 3 vols, facs. edn (New York, 1967), vol. II, p. 705.

6 Jurgis Baltrušaitis, *Le Moyen-âge fantastique* (Paris, 1993), pp. 155–202.

7 S. Kusukawa, 'The Sources of Gesner's *Historia animalium*', *Annals of Science*, LXVII/3 (2010), pp. 326–7.

8 A. R. Radcliffe-Brown, 'The Rainbow-serpent Myth of Australia', *Journal of the Royal Anthropological Institute of Great Britain and Ireland*, LVI (1929), pp. 19–25.

9 A. W. Reed, *Aboriginal Myths: Tales of Dreamtime* (Sydney, 2000), pp. 106–8.

10 Marty Crump, *Eye of Newt and Toe of Frog, Adder's Fork and Lizard's Leg: The Lore and Mythology of Amphibians and Reptiles* (Chicago, IL, 2015), p. 35.

11 Dennis Tedlock, *Popol Vuh: The Mayan Book of the Dawn of Life*, rev. edn (New York, 1996), pp. 147–9.

12 Pedro Pitrarch, *The Jaguar and the Priest: An Ethnography of Tzeltal Souls* (Austin, TX, 2010), pp. 1–5.

13 James George Frazier, *Myths of the Origin of Fire: An Essay* [1930] (Reddich, 2010), chap. XII.

14 Judy Allen and Jeanne Griffiths, *The Book of the Dragon* (Secaucus, NJ, 1979), pp. 60–61.

15 Anne van Cutsem-Vanderstraete, 'Parures animales: Dialogue entre formes et matières', in *Animal*, ed. Christiane Falgayrettes-Leveau (Paris, 2007), pp. 384, 397.

16 Brian Morris, *Animals and Ancestors: An Ethnography* (Oxford, 2000), pp. 279–81.

17 Jan Knappert, *African Mythology* (London, 1995), p. 261.

18 Morris, *Animals and Ancestors*, p. 180.

19 Viviane Baeke, 'Les Hommes et leurs "doublures" animales', in *Animal*, ed. Falgayrettes-Leveau, pp. 286–8.

20 Carolyn Wells, 'How to Know the Wild Animals', in *The Wit and Humor of America*, ed. Marshall P. Wilder (New York, 1911), vol. IV, pp. 92–3.

4 LIZARDS AND DINOSAURS

1 R. C. Zaehner, *The Teachings of the Magi: A Compendium of Zoroastrian Beliefs* (New York, 1956), p. 47.
2 John Noble Wilford, *The Riddle of the Dinosaurs* (New York, 1985), pp. 59–60.
3 Donald Worster, *Nature's Economy: A History of Ecological Ideas*, 2nd edn (Cambridge, 1994), p. 126.
4 Ibid., p. 139.
5 Thomas Hawkins, *The Book of Great Sea Dragons, Ichthyosauri and Plesiosauri* (London, 1840), p. 3.
6 Ibid., p. 27.
7 Alfred, Lord Tennyson, *The Complete Poetical Works of Tennyson* (Cambridge, MA, 1898), p. 176.
8 Gideon Mantell, *Wonders of Geology: or, A Familiar Exposition of Geological Phenomena* (London, 1839), vol. I, p. 400.
9 Steve McCarthy, *The Crystal Palace Dinosaurs: The Story of the World's First Prehistoric Sculptures* (London, 1994), p. 10.
10 Samuel Phillips, *Guide to the Crystal Palace and Park* [1865], facs. edn (London, 2008), p. 193.
11 McCarthy, *Crystal Palace Dinosaurs*, p. 137.
12 Ibid., p. 22.
13 Ibid., p. 27.
14 Ibid., p. 22.
15 Jules Verne, *Journey to the Center of the Earth* [1864] (New York, 2005), pp. 175–6.
16 David Norman, *Dinosaurs: A Very Short Introduction* (Oxford, 2005), p. 120.
17 Wilford, *Riddle of the Dinosaurs*, pp. 162–8.
18 Emily Anthes, 'Coldblooded Does Not Mean Stupid', *New York Times* (13 November 2013), p. D1.

19 Marty Crump, *Eye of Newt and Toe of Frog, Adder's Fork and Lizard's Leg: The Lore and Mythology of Amphibians and Reptiles* (Chicago, IL, 2015), p. 18.

20 Michael Crichton, *Jurassic Park* (New York, 1990).

21 Michael Crichton, *The Lost World* (New York, 1995).

22 Judy Allen and Jeanne Griffiths, *The Book of the Dragon* (Secaucus, NJ, 1979), p. 119.

23 Carl Sagan, *Dragons of Eden: Speculations on the Evolution of Human Intelligence* (New York, 1977), p. 151.

5 THE LIZARD IN ART

1 Lorenzo Lorenzi, *Devils in Art: Florence, from the Middle Ages to the Renaissance,* trans. Mark Roberts (Perugia, 2006), p. 130.

2 Physiologus, *Physiologus,* trans. Michael J. Curley (Austin, TX, 1979), pp. 66–7.

3 Alan Gibbon, *Céramiques de Bernard Palissy* (Paris, 1986), p. 29.

4 William R. Newman, *Promethean Ambitions: Alchemy and the Quest to Perfect Nature* (Chicago, IL, 2004), pp. 145–63.

5 Marshall P. Katz and Robert Lehr, *Palissy Ware: Nineteenth-century French Ceramists from Avisseau to Renoleau* (London, 1996), pp. 44–61.

6 Jack Goody, *The Culture of Flowers* (Cambridge, 1994), p. 177.

7 Sybille Ebert-Schifferer, *Still Life: A History*, trans. Russell Stockman (New York, 1999), p. 115.

8 Ibid., p. 111.

9 David Badger, *Lizards: A Natural History of Some Uncommon Creatures – Extraordinary Chameleons, Iguanas, Geckos and More* (St Paul, MN, 2002), p. 148.

6 LIZARDS TODAY

1 Vinciane Despret, *Que diraient les animaux, si . . . on leur posait les bonnes questions?* (Paris, 2014), p. 63.

2 Elizabeth Kolbert, *The Sixth Extinction: An Unnatural History* (New York, 2014), p. 21.

3 David Badger, *Lizards: A Natural History of Some Uncommon Creatures – Extraordinary Chameleons, Iguanas, Geckos and More* (St Paul, MN, 2002), pp. 147–8.

4 David Attenborough, *Life in Cold Blood* (Princeton, NJ, 2008), p. 281.

Select Bibliography

Allen, Judy, and Jeanne Griffiths, *The Book of the Dragon* (Secaucus, NJ, 1979)

Anthes, Emily, 'Coldblooded Does Not Mean Stupid', *New York Times* (13 November 2013), p. D1

Attenborough, David, *Life in Cold Blood* (Princeton, NJ, 2008)

Badger, David, *Lizards: A Natural History of Some Uncommon Creatures – Extraordinary Chameleons, Iguanas, Geckos and More* (St Paul, MN, 2002)

Baeke, Viviane, 'Les Hommes et leurs "doublures" animales', *Animal*, ed. Christiane Falgayrettes-Leveau (Paris, 2007), pp. 253–98

Baltrušaitis, Jurgis, *Le Moyen-âge fantastique* (Paris, 1993)

Barber, Richard, *Bestiary* (Woodridge, 1993)

Berlin, Brent, *Ethnobiological Classification: Principles of Classification of Plants and Animals in Traditional Societies* (Princeton, NJ, 1992)

—, 'The First Congress of Ethnozoological Nomenclature', *Journal of the Royal Anthropological Institute*, XII/1 (London, 2006), pp. 23–44

de Buffon, Georges Louis, Comte, *Buffon's Natural History* (London, 1792), vol. VI

Burkert, Walter, *Creation of the Sacred: Tracks of Biology in Early Religions* (Cambridge, MA, 1966)

Crichton, Michael, *Jurassic Park* (New York, 1990)

—, *The Lost World* (New York, 1995)

Crump, Marty, *Eye of Newt and Toe of Frog, Adder's Fork and Lizard's Leg: The Lore and Mythology of Amphibians and Reptiles* (Chicago, IL, 2015)

Cutsem-Vanderstraete, Anne van, 'Parures animales: Dialogue entre formes et matières', in *Animal*, ed. Christiane Falgayrettes-Leveau (Paris, 2007), pp. 377–420

Desmond, Ray, *Wonders of Creation: Natural History Drawings in the British Library* (London, 1986)

Despret, Vinciane, *Que diraient les animaux, si . . . on leur posait les bonnes questions?* (Paris, 2014)

Douglas, Mary, *Purity and Danger: An Analysis of Concepts of Pollution and Taboo* [1966] (London, 2003)

Ebert-Schifferer, Sybille, *Still Life: A History*, trans. Russell Stockman (New York, 1999)

Forth, Gregory, 'Symbolic Lizards: Forms of Special Purpose Classification of Animals among the Nage of Eastern Indonesia', *Anthrozoös*, XXVI/3 (Cambridge, 2013), pp. 357–72

Frazier, James George, *Myths of the Origin of Fire: An Essay* [1930] (Redditch, 2010)

Gebhard, Harold, and Maria Ludwig, *Von Drachen, Yetis, und Vampiren: Fabeltieren auf der Spur* (Munich, 2005)

Gibbon, Alan, *Céramiques de Bernard Palissy* (Paris, 1986)

Goldsmith, Oliver, *History of Animated Nature* [1774] (Cheapside, 1838), vol. IV

Goodrich, S. G., *Johnson's Natural History*, 2 vols (New York, 1859, 1867)

Goody, Jack, *The Culture of Flowers* (Cambridge, 1994)

Hawkins, Thomas, *The Book of Great Sea Dragons, Ichthyosauri and Plesiosauri* (London, 1840)

Katz, Marshall P., and Robert Lehr, *Palissy Ware: Nineteenth-century French Ceramists from Avisseau to Renoleau* (London, 1996)

Knappert, Jan, *African Mythology* (London, 1995)

Kolbert, Elizabeth, *The Sixth Extinction: An Unnatural History* (New York, 2014)

Kusukawa, S., 'The Sources of Gesner's Historia Animalium', *Annals of Science*, LXVII/3 (2010), pp. 303–28

Lippincott, Louise, and Andreas Blühm, *Fierce Friends: Artists and Animals, 1750–1900* (London, 2005)

Lorenzi, Lorenzo, *Devils in Art: Florence, from the Middle Ages to the Renaissance,* trans. Mark Roberts (Perugia, 2006)

McCarthy, Steve, *The Crystal Palace Dinosaurs: The Story of the World's First Prehistoric Sculptures* (London, 1994)

Mantell, Gideon, *Wonders of Geology: or, A Familiar Exposition of Geological Phenomena,* vol. I (London, 1839)

Mattison, Chris, *Lizards of the World* (New York, 1989)

Melville, Herman, *Moby Dick, or The Whale* [1851] (New York, 1902)

Morris, Brian, *Animals and Ancestors: An Ethnography* (Oxford, 2000)

Newman, William R., *Promethean Ambitions: Alchemy and the Quest to Perfect Nature* (Chicago, IL, 2004)

Norman, David, *Dinosaurs: A Very Short Introduction* (Oxford, 2005)

Pennant, Thomas, *History of Quadrupeds,* 2 vols (London, 1793)

Phillips, Samuel, *Guide to the Crystal Palace and Park* [1856], facs. edn (London, 2008)

Physiologus, *Physiologus,* trans. Michael J. Curley (Austin, TX, 1979)

Pianka, Eric R., and Laurie J. Vitt, *Lizards: Windows to the Evolution of Diversity* (Oakland, CA, 2003)

Pitrarch, Pedro, *The Jaguar and the Priest: An Ethnography of Tzeltal Souls* (Austin, TX, 2010)

Radcliffe-Brown, A. R., 'The Rainbow-Serpent Myth of Australia', *Journal of the Royal Anthropological Institute of Great Britain and Ireland,* LVI (1929), pp. 19–25

Reed, A. W., *Aboriginal Myths: Tales of Dreamtime* (Sydney, 2000)

Ritvo, Harriet, *The Platypus and the Mermaid, and Other Figments of the Classifying Imagination* (Cambridge, MA, 1997)

Sagan, Carl, *Dragons of Eden: Speculations on the Evolution of Human Intelligence* (New York, 1977)

Sterckx, Roel, *The Animal and Demon in Early Modern China* (Albany, NY, 2002)

Tedlock, Dennis, *Popol Vuh: The Mayan Book of the Dawn of Life,* revd edn (New York, 1996)

Tennyson, Alfred, Lord, *The Complete Poetical Works of Tennyson* (Cambridge, MA, 1898)

Teyssier, Jérémie, Suzanne V. Saenko, Dirk van der Marel and Michel C. Milinkovitch, 'Photonic Crystals Cause Active Colour Change in Chameleons', *Nature Communications*, 6 (March 2015), www.nature.com, accessed 2 December 2015

Toperoff, Shlomo Pesach, *The Animal Kingdom in Jewish Thought* (London, 1995)

Topsell, Edward, and Thomas Muffet, *The History of Four-footed Beasts and Serpents and Insects* [1658], facs. edn, 3 vols (New York, 1967)

Verne, Jules, *Journey to the Center of the Earth* [1864] (New York, 2005)

Wells, Carolyn, 'How to Know the Wild Animals', in *The Wit and Humor of America*, ed. Marshall P. Wilder (New York, 1911), vol. IV, pp. 92–3

Wilford, John Noble, *The Riddle of the Dinosaurs* (New York, 1985)

Worster, Donald, *Nature's Economy: A History of Ecological Ideas*, 2nd edn (Cambridge, 1994)

Yoon, Carol Kaesuk, *Naming Nature: The Clash between Instinct and Science* (New York, 2009)

Zaehner, R. C., *The Teachings of the Magi: A Compendium of Zoroastrian Beliefs* (New York, 1956)

Associations and Websites

AMERICAN MUSEUM OF NATURAL HISTORY
www.amnh.org/exhibitions/mythic-creatures/dragons-creatures-of-power/natural-history-of-dragons
Extensive material on dragons, combining natural history, anthropology and folklore.

THE BIODIVERSITY GROUP, REPTILES
www.biodiversitygroup.org/reptiles
A website centred primarily around the threats that lizards and other creatures are facing in the Anthropocene.

BIOINTERACTIVE
www.hhmi.org/biointeractive/origin-species-lizards-evolutionary-tree
A site primarily for teachers, offering mostly free resources for teaching science, including many for herpetology.

CALIFORNIA HERPS
www.californiaherps.com
This is an extensive guide to lizards and other reptiles of California, which also contains a rather humorous section on lizards in the movies.

CRYSTAL PALACE DINOSAURS
http://cpdinosaurs.org
A beautifully illustrated site devoted to the history and conservation of the Crystal Palace Dinosaurs.

DINOSAUR DATABASE
www.dinodatabase.com
A website with extensive information about almost everything pertaining to dinosaurs, including their lives, classification and discovery, with extensive links to museums and centres of research.

LIVE SCIENCE, DRAGONS
www.livescience.com/25559-dragons.html
A site with many useful links devoted to mythic dragons and the documented creatures that may be their foundation.

NATIONAL GEOGRAPHIC SOCIETY
http://animals.nationalgeographic.com
A popular source for news and other material pertaining to zoology, with extensive sections on both dinosaurs and living reptiles.

REPTILES MAGAZINE
www.reptilesmagazine.com/lizards
The website of a popular publication that specializes in the acquisition and care of pet reptiles, and also has a great deal of material on recent developments in herpetology. It contains a very extensive section on lizards.

Acknowledgements

I would like to thank my wife, Linda Sax, for her emotional support in writing this book, which has, at times, kept me from many other activities that might have been more immediately useful or entertaining. Many people would have thought the idea of writing a cultural history of lizards a bit eccentric, but she always appreciated it. She also provided an important service by reading chapters in progress and making many helpful suggestions.

Thanks also go to the people at Reaktion Books, particularly to Jonathan Burt and Michael R. Leaman, for their confidence in this book. Bryan Talbot, author of the *Grandville* series of graphic novels, generously allowed me to reproduce pictures depicting lizards from his work. I have used some illustrations that were made available copyright-free by the institutions at www.openculture.com. Especially useful to me have been those of the Metropolitan Museum of Art in New York, the Solomon R. Guggenheim Museum in New York, the Rijksmuseum in Amsterdam, the National Gallery in Washington and the John Paul Getty Museum in Los Angeles. Also very helpful has been the Wikipedia Commons.

Some of the illustrations are from my own private collection, consisting mostly of pictures that I have picked up at flea markets. Looking through stacks of old pictures at an outdoor stall may, in ways, not be the most efficient way to obtain illustrations, but it is wonderful fun and provides great opportunities for serendipity. Special thanks go to Phyllis Newman at the Green Flea Market in Manhattan, who often helped me look for pictures and gave me some very good deals. I have also purchased a number of graphics at www.fotosearch.com and from the Pictorial Archive series from Dover Books.

Perhaps every project is more of a collective effort than we usually appreciate. We constantly absorb suggestions, hints and fragmentary ideas from others, and then process these in ways that we ourselves may not be aware of. I cannot list all who may have contributed in some way to this book, but, as the poet W. B. Yeats put it in 'Gratitude to Unknown Instructors',

All things hang like a drop of dew
Upon a blade of grass.

That is something that lizards would understand.

Photo Acknowledgements

The author and publishers wish to express their thanks to the below sources of illustrative material and/or permission to reproduce it.

© Angela N. Perryman/shutterstock.com: p. 37 (bottom); © Ariadna126/ www.fotosearch.com: p. 84; photos author: pp. 9, 14 (top and bottom), 20, 36 (top), 38 (top), 41, 46, 55, 69 (top), 70, 111, 125 (top), 157, 160 (top and bottom); Spencer Fullerton Baird, ed., *The Iconographic Encyclopedia* (London, 1857): p. 120; © Bernhard Richter/www.shutterstock.com: p. 37 (top); © Bobonacus/ www.fotosearch.com: p. 29; photos British Library: p. 119; Carl Joseph Brodtmann, *Naturhistorische Bilder-Gallerie aus dem Thierreiche* (Berlin, 1816): p. 19; George Louis Leclerc, Comte de Buffon, *Histoire naturelle* (Paris, 1749–1804): p. 47; © CathyKeifer/ www.fotosearch.com: pp. 33, 43, 68, 93; Ephraim Chambers, *Cyclopædia: or, a Universal Dictionary of Arts and Sciences* (London, 1728): p. 67; photos Museo Nazionale del Cinema, Turin: p. 125; collection of the author: pp. 52, 85, 90, 98, 113, 114, 124; William Daniel, *Oriental Scenery* (London, 1807): p. 38 (bottom); Leopold Joseph Fitzinger, *Bilder-Atlas zur Wissenschaftlich-populären Naturgeschichte der Wirbeltiere* (Vienna, 1867): p. 51; © Friedemeier/www.fotosearch.com: p. 32 (top); Conrad Gessner, *Historia animalium* (Zürich, 1669): p. 79; courtesy of the J. Paul Getty Museum, Los Angeles (Open Content Program): pp. 18, 142, 145 (bottom); Oliver Goldsmith, *A History of the Earth and Animated Nature* (London, 1774): pp. 17, 22; photos Google Art Project, Birmingham Museum of Art, Birmingham, Alabama: p. 146; J. J. Grandville, *Les Fleurs animées* (Paris, 1867): p. 152; Félix Édouard Guérin-Méneville, *Dictionnaire*

pittoresque d'histoire naturelle (Paris, 1839): p. 101; © Hagen411/www.
fotosearch.com: p. 78; Thomas Hawkins, *The Book of Great Sea Dragons,
Ichthyosauri and Plesiosauri* (London, 1840): p. 106; Pierre-Jules Hetzel,
ed., *Scènes de la vie privée et publique des animaux* (Paris, 1840–42):
pp. 12, 56, 95; © JakeDany/www.fotosearch.com: p. 59; © jasoncheever/
www.fotosearch.com: p. 89; A. J. Johnson, *Johnson's Natural History*
(New York, 1867): p. 115; photos Kunsthistorisches Museum, Vienna:
p. 133; © LanaLanglois/www.fotosearch.com: p. 40; © John Leech:
p. 112; © Leekrob/www.fotosearch.com: p. 41 (top); photos Fondazione
Roberto Longhi, Florence: p. 150; Michael Maier, *Secretorum Chymicum
. . .* (Frankfurt, 1687): p. 80; photos Museum Mayer van den Bergh,
Antwerp, Belgium: pp. 136 (top and bottom), 139; Mathurin Méheut,
Études d'animaux (Paris, 1911): p. 154; photos Metropolitan Museum
of Art: pp. 69 (bottom), 73, 130, 132, 140, 141, 145 (top); Adolphe
Millot, *Nouveau Larousse illustré* (Paris, 1897–1904): p. 21; © Miro Vrlik/
Photography/shutterstock.com: p. 35; © Mollynz/www.fotosearch.com:
p. 57; © Morphart/www.fotosearch.com: p. 116; © The National Gallery,
London: p. 75; photos National Gallery of Art, Washington, DC: p. 164;
photos Museum of New Zealand Te Papa Tongarewa, Wellington: p. 109,
© Olga sweet/www.fotosearch.com: p. 66; © ohrim/Shutterstock.com:
p. 88; © Photomaru/www.fotosearch.com: p. 42; photos Museo Nacional
Del Prado, Madrid: p. 134; Antoine-François Prévost, *Histoire générale
des voyages* (Paris, 1746–59): pp. 13, 25; private collection: pp. 149, 153; ©
Rdodson/www.fotosearch.com: p. 50; © Reptiles4all/shutterstock.
com: p. 48; courtesy of the Rijksmuseum, Amsterdam: pp. 92, 93 (top
and bottom), 143, 147; © Rogdeg/www.fotosearch.com: p. 39; *Journal of
the Royal Anthropological Association*, LVI (1926): p. 82 (top and bottom):
p. 83; © Ryan M. Bolton/shutterstock.com: p. 49; G. H. von Schubert,
Natural History of the Animal Kingdom for School and Home (London,
1889): p. 16; Albertus Seba, *Locupletissimi rerum naturalium thesauri
accurata descriptio* (*c.* 1734–65): pp. 44, 58; Anton Seder, *Das Thier in der
decorativen Kunst* (Vienna, 1896): p. 155; © SlidePix/www.fotosearch.
com: p. 34; © StrangerView/www.fotosearch.com: p. 65; © Bryan Talbot:
pp. 54, 123; Toho Company Ltd. (東宝株式会社, Tōhō Kabushiki-
kaisha) © 1954: p. 117; Edward Topsell, *History of Four-footed Beasts and*

Index